DORYX®
(coated doxycycline
hyclate pellets)

The [...] .ent

Professional (PMP)

Exam Guide

Brent W. Knapp, PMP®

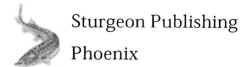

Sturgeon Publishing
Phoenix

COPYRIGHT INFORMATION

Published by: Sturgeon Pubishing in association with www.pmptools.com, inc.

Email: publishing@pmptools.com

Library of Congress Control Number: 2003095560

ISBN 0-9726656-1-7 (paperback)

Manufactured in the United States of America

10 9 8 7 6 5 4 3 2 1

Table of Contents

Chapter 6 - Project Cost Management

Chapter 7 - Project Quality Management

Chapter 8 - Project Human Resource Management

Chapter 9 - Project Communications Management

Chapter 10 - Project Risk Management

INTRODUCTION

. . . .

WHAT IS PMP CERTIFICATION?

The Project Management Institute (PMI) offers certification as a Project Management Professional (PMP). More detailed information is available from PMI in a brochure called "Certification & Standards" and is available on the web at www.pmi.org.

PMI conducts a certification program in project management. PMI's Project Management Professional (PMP) certification is the project management profession's most globally recognized and respected certification credential. To obtain PMP certification an individual must satisfy education and experience requirements, agree to and adhere to a Code of Professional Conduct, and pass the PMP Certification Examination.

Worldwide there are more than 50,000 PMP's who provide project management services in 26 countries. Many corporations now require PMP certification for individual advancement within the corporation or for employment.

REQUIREMENTS FOR EARNING PMP CERTIFICATION?

There are four main requirements for earning PMP certification:

- Having experience working in the field of project management—4,500 hours with a baccalaureate degree and 7,500 without a degree.
- Signing a PMP Candidate Agreement and Release form.
- Completing the PMP Certification Exam Application
- Paying a fee of $555 for non-PMI members and $405 for members.

REQUIREMENTS FOR MAINTAINING PMP CERTIFICATION?

In January 1999, PMI started a new professional development program for maintaining the PMP certification. You must earn at least sixty Professional Development Units within a three-year cycle and adhere to PMI's PMP Code of Professional Conduct. You may want to consult the PMI Web site at http://www.pmi.org for more details.

STRUCTURE AND CONTENT OF THE PMP CERTIFICATION EXAM

The PMP exam consists of 200 multiple-choice questions that test your knowledge in the nine PMBOK Guide knowledge areas of Integration, Scope, Time, Cost, Quality, Human Resource, Communications, Risk, and Procurement; the five PMBOK process groups of Project Initiation, Project Planning, Project Execution, Project Control, and Project Closing; and the area of Professional Responsibility. The exam can be difficult, not because of the nature of the subject matter (which is actually quite basic), but because—

- Some questions are awkwardly worded and ambiguous; sometimes it is difficult to determine exactly what the test writer is asking
- Some questions tend to test one's memory of specific language (that is, definition and terms) from the PMBOK Guide, PMI publications, and other reference materials
- Many questions take an activity that could legitimately be done many different ways and ask you to choose the "best way", or "what is the first step" you would take given a particular situation.

The exam is mostly qualitative, not quantitative, and many of the quantitative questions are not that difficult. However, most exam takers seem to find the most problems with questions that address quality, cost, and risk topics. The quality questions are difficult for many people because they have learned a philosophy and practice of quality in their organizations that are somewhat different from that espoused by PMI even though PMI's approach is consistent with many of the "gurus" in the field. The questions that address cost topics tend to cover a breadth of material much more diverse than the average test-taker has previously been exposed to. For example, in addition to having to know all the earned-value formulas, one needs to know a variety of information from benefit-cost ratio to understanding the two methods of capital depreciation.

HOW TO PREPARE FOR THE PMP EXAM?

Like most people, you have probably developed your own study habits through the years, and you know what works best for you. I am not suggesting that I have identified the only way to study for this rigorous undertaking. In fact, there are several ways to approach this, which when combined with individual study can have powerful results. But I have identified some approaches over the years that seem to produce good results.

- Do a little every day. Do not wait until the week before the exam to start studying. You are already too late.
- Prepare for the exam with other test-takers. Studying with other people provides a powerful advantage enabling you to learn more information faster. Plan on lunch-hour sessions, if convenient, or before or-after-work sessions.

- Within your group, you can create a division of labor where different persons are responsible for teaching the subject matter in specific sections of the PMBOK Guide to others in the group.
- Perhaps the most powerful of all approaches is to review in your group every practice test question you received. The process of discussing among yourselves how you selected your answer and what rationale you used for each answer is an extremely productive one. We guarantee that this group study method will, in all likelihood, result in your learning more about project management concepts and practice than any individual study method.
- Ask people questions who have taken the exam. Get as much input as possible. Do not limit your questions to those who have passed the exam. If possible, ask those who have failed the exam what their experiences were.

ONE MONTH BEFORE THE EXAM

You do not have much time. You should be taking and retaking the practice test, studying the PMP® Simulated Test Bank, and working with your study group (if possible). Keep track of the questions and definitions you are answering right and those you are getting wrong. Make sure you are studying a little every day.

Concentrate on those areas in which you are having problems. Spend a minimum of one hour each day in your three weakest areas. Implement the study strategies you know work best for you (should you answer all the easy questions first, the harder ones, or skip around, or some other approach?) Write down your approaches and practice them.

Using whatever format and approach you find helpful, go over at least ten new definitions every day.

ONE WEEK BEFORE THE EXAM

Continue to work through the practice questions (by Knowledge Area) and any practice test you may have. Also on a daily basis, start reviewing definitions.

EXAM DAY

Think confidently! Do not dwell on your weaknesses; concentrate on your strengths. You have been studying very hard, you are prepared, and you know what to expect.

TIPS FOR TAKING THE PMP EXAM

- Make sure you have everything you need remember that pencils and calculators are usually provided. You will not be allowed to bring any additional items in with you.
- Listen carefully to the proctor's directions and comments as you do not want to make any procedural errors; it can result in lost time and possibly wrong answers.
- Review the exam, reading the directions carefully. Do not start answering the questions before you read the directions on the screen.
- Try and budget your time as you have a little more than a minute for each question. Realistically, you can answer some questions in a few seconds, and others will take several minutes to answer. Be mindful of the time you are spending in each section, but do not be obsessed with it. Very few people run out of time.
- Write down important formulas, facts, and statistics in the margin or on scratch paper as soon as you sit down. This can be done during the computer tutorial. This safeguard will ensure that you do not forget certain information if you become too nervous.
- Look for "qualifying" words in the stem of the question or in the answers. For example, words such as, rarely, often, seldom, many, always, and so on will determine the correct answer.
- Answer the easy questions first. A good way to reduce anxiety is to answer the easy questions first. This will build your confidence as you proceed through the rest of the exam section. If you attempt the more difficult questions initially, you will tend to feel uninformed, unprepared, and "unhappy."
- If you do not know the answer, mark (electronically or otherwise) the question and complete it later. There will be many questions for which the answer will not be immediately apparent. Rather than struggle with the question, move on to the next one. Return to those unanswered questions later. Chances are your memory will return, and you will be able to make a better educated guess the second or third time you read the question.
- Guess aggressively. Never leave a question blank. You are scored on the number of correct answers; points are not deducted for wrong answers.
- Use all the time allowed. If you finish early, check for errors. Review the directions once again to ensure that you have followed them correctly.
- Try not to think about your score while taking the exam. Thinking about your score will not raise it; thinking about the answers will!

PROJECT FRAMEWORK

. . . .

GUIDE TO THE PROJECT MANAGEMENT BODY OF KNOWLEDGE (PMBOK GUIDE)

The Guide to the Project Management Body of Knowledge (PMBOK Guide) is a term that describes the sum of knowledge within the profession of project management. The body of knowledge rests with the professionals and academics that apply and advance it.

The Guide to the Project Management Body of Knowledge (PMBOK Guide) describes a subset of the PMBOK that is generally accepted, meaning that the knowledge and practices are applicable to most projects most of the time, and there is a widespread consensus about their value and usefulness. The text is published by the Project Management Institute, which is recognized as the authoritative association for project managers. Based on stringent requirements for project management experience, academic education, and a rigorous testing program, PMI certifies individuals as Project Management Professionals (PMP), the most recognized certification for project managers in the business world today.

WHAT IS A PROJECT?

A project is a temporary sequence of tasks with a distinct beginning and an end that is undertaken to create a unique product or service. In addition, a project must have defined objectives in order to clearly indicate when the project has been completed. There are some necessary features that characterize all projects:

- Projects follow an organized process in order to meet specific goals.
- Project goals are based on specific quality standards.
- Projects use time, money, resources, and people that are allocated to the project.
- Projects have a distinct beginning and end.
- Projects generally have time and cost constraints.
- Projects are usually completed by a team of people.

There are several attributes that characterize a project:

- Projects are unique. The product or service being produced by the project is different and involves doing something that has not been done before.
- Projects have a purpose. Projects have a well-defined set of desired results. They can be divided into smaller tasks in order to achieve the overall project goal.

2

- Projects have a life cycle. Projects progress from an idea through the planning, executing, and controlling steps, and finally to a close. The project life cycle also indicates that projects are temporary, with a definite beginning and a definite end.
- Projects have interdependencies. The various tasks of a project interact with one another, while at the same time interacting with the parent organization.

Projects are temporary in nature, while operations are ongoing. Projects have definitive start dates and definitive end dates. Operations involve work that is continuous without an ending date and most often repeat the same process.

WHAT IS PROJECT MANAGEMENT?

Project management is a method and a set of techniques based on the accepted principles of management used for planning, estimating, and controlling work activities to reach a desired end result on time, within budget, and according to specifications.

PROJECT MANAGEMENT KNOWLEDGE AREAS

Listed below are the nine project management knowledge areas:

PROJECT INTEGRATION MANAGEMENT

Integration Management skills are used to integrate the work in other core areas. The primary focus of integration management is the creation of a cohesive, comprehensive, and well-designed project plan and the execution of that project plan. Another skill is the overseeing of the change control process, both as it is developed in the plan and as it is executed throughout the life of the project.

PROJECT SCOPE MANAGEMENT

Scope Management is the skill project managers use to define the work that needs to be done on any given project. This entails making sure that all the work required is included and that no unneeded work is added. It includes formal project and phase initiations, developing the written scope statement (with scope exclusions), and listing major and intermediary project deliverables. It also includes the formal agreement by major players to the scope as defined and scope change control (the ongoing process of evaluating project changes).

PROJECT TIME MANAGEMENT

Time Management is the skill that most people associate with project management because it is crucial for keeping on schedule. It includes creating or refining the project work breakdown structure, determining dependency relationships among the project tasks, estimating the effort and duration of the tasks, and creating a project schedule. It also includes the control component of monitoring and updating the project progress and making changes to estimates and schedules.

A commonly misunderstood facet of project management is that, by the nature of projects, estimates and schedules will change. As long as the project manager stays on top of these changes, this should not affect the final target completion date.

PROJECT COST MANAGEMENT

Cost Management includes determining the project cost categories, estimating the use of each resource in each category, budgeting for that estimated cost and getting it approved, and then controlling the cost as the project progresses. Both fixed costs (such as equipment and software purchases) and variable costs (such as team member time) are included in the planning and estimating and are then monitored and controlled.

PROJECT QUALITY MANAGEMENT

Quality Management has three subsets, generally referred to as Quality Planning, Quality Assurance, and Quality Control. In Quality Planning, a project manager defines what represents quality and how quality will be measured. In Quality Assurance, the project manager watches the overall quality of a project to see that standards will be met. In Quality Control, the project manager examines actual project outputs to evaluate their conformance to the standards set in the plan.

PROJECT HUMAN RESOURCE MANAGEMENT

Human Resource Management addresses the people involved in a project. It includes the planning components of determining what skills are needed to perform the various project tasks, defining the participants' roles and responsibilities, and selecting potential candidates for those tasks. It also includes acquiring the appropriate resources (internally, from external departments, or even external companies or independent contractors) and any professional development that the team members may need to improve their project performance.

PROJECT COMMUNICATIONS MANAGEMENT

Communication Management is the often neglected, yet perhaps most important, component of project management. It includes deciding who needs what information, to what level of detail, and in what media and time period. These needs are documented in the communication plan subsection of the project plan so that parties can review them and then follow them. The communication plan may also specify the format to be used for each communication, as well as turnaround times for each communication. Once the plan is approved, project managers then use their communication management skills to make sure the information is gathered and distributed according to the plan.

PROJECT RISK MANAGEMENT

Risk Management starts with identifying the potential risks to a project and then determining the likelihood of each risk happening and how that risk would impact the project if it occurred. From this list and ranking, contingencies are developed for the highest risks. As the project is executed, one can use these contingencies to regain control of a project if a potential risk does occur.

PROJECT PROCUREMENT MANAGEMENT

Procurement Management involves developing, executing, and monitoring contracts with service and product vendors. It also includes deciding what must be procured, soliciting bids for the products or services, selecting the appropriate vendor, and closing the contract once the project has been completed.

RELATIONSHIP TO OTHER MANAGEMENT DISCIPLINES

Most of the knowledge and skills that a project manager needs are unique to the project management process. For example, general managers would not ordinarily need to complete a critical path analysis or understand how to put a project on the fast track.

However, there are some areas of overlap between general management and project management, such as planning the project, staffing a department, and executing a task.

PROGRAMS

The terms project and program are often used interchangeably. Although these terms are related, they are not the same thing. A program is a group of logically related projects. Likewise, projects are managed together in order to gain benefits that are not available from managing them separately, or because they include similar processes that will benefit from simultaneous management.

SUB-PROJECTS

Very large projects may be divided into several sub-projects, each of which is a project in its own right. This division makes for better management control. For example, sub-projects can be defined at the department, division, or geographic level.

This artificial decomposition of a complex project into subprojects often simplifies the scheduling of resources and reduces the need for interdepartmental communications while a specific activity is worked on. The downside to dividing a project into sub-projects is that the projects are now interdependent.

PROJECT PHASES AND PROJECT LIFE CYCLE

Projects are unique and subject to risk. Thus, dividing a project into to several parts called 'phases' allows better control and appropriate links to the ongoing operations. When grouped together, project phases are referred to as a "project life cycle."

PROJECT PHASES

Every project phase is associated with one or more deliverables upon completion. A deliverable is a tangible, verifiable work product and would generally follow sequentially in the development of a product of the project.

The end of a project phase should be linked with a review of key deliverables and project performance to:

- Decide if the project should move into the next phase.
- Recognize and rectify errors cost effectively.

These reviews are referred to phase exits, stage gates, or kill points.

PROJECT LIFE CYCLES

The project life cycle defines the beginning and end of a project and determines which transitional actions are included at the end of a project, linking the project to the ongoing operations.

Typically, a handoff will occur between project phases of the life cycle, and deliverables from the preceding phase should be approved before moving forward. However, in some cases, a subsequent phase will begin prior to completion of a preceding phase, a practice called fast tracking.

Some life cycles may be called a "project management methodology" where a disciplined, highly detailed approach is applied. Most life cycles share some common traits:

- Project cost and initial staffing are low at the start, increase towards the middle and near the end of a project, and drop off rapidly at the end.
- Risk and uncertainty are at their peak at the beginning of a project and gradually diminish as the project continues.
- The ability of stakeholders to persuade or influence the final characteristics of the project product and final cost are highest at the start of a project and diminish as the project continues.
- The cost of changes and error correction generally increases as the project continues.

Remember, a project life cycle is not the same as a product life cycle. A product life cycle will normally include the project life cycle as a subset of the overall product life cycle. The product life cycle will encompass the development, deployment, support, maintenance, upgrades (which may be a separate project), and eventual shutdown of the given product.

PROJECT STAKEHOLDERS

A project stakeholder is an individual, group, or organization that is involved in a project, whose interests might be influenced as a result of project's achievement. It is important for the project manager or the project team to identify the stakeholders and their expectations. In addition, it is important to manage the stakeholders' expectations in order to reduce conflict. The key stakeholders in every project include:

- The project manager, because this individual is in charge of successful project completion.
- The project team, because these are the individuals most directly involved in completing the work of the project.
- The public is sometimes considered a stakeholder because they might be affected by the outcome of the project.
- The parent organization, because it provides the employees who work on the project.
- The customer, because this is the individual or organization that will use the product created by the project.

ORGANIZATIONAL INFLUENCES

Most projects are a smaller part of a larger organization, and this organization will have significant influence on the conduct and success or failure of the project. There are three primary organizational influences that can affect project management:

- The organizational values, beliefs, and expectations can either be adopted or rejected by the project team, having a direct effect on the management of a project.
- The structure of an organization can affect project management because it can dictate the availability of resources such as money and staff.
- The organization's project philosophy can affect project management, since a project-based organization would reward different actions than a non-profit-based organization.

ORGANIZATIONAL SYSTEMS

Project-based organizations operations are primarily projects. This would include organizations whose main source of revenue is projects (consultants, contractors) and organizations that manage by projects.

Non-project based organizations are more focused on operations, and seldom have management systems to facilitate project needs efficiently. This complicates the project management effort.

The Project Management Professional (PMP®) Exam Guide

ORGANIZATIONAL CULTURES AND STYLE

Obviously, each organization has developed its own culture and style, and the project teams must consider this. For example, a team suggesting a high—risk approach will more likely receive sponsorship in an entrepreneurial organization that may not have an established style. A project manager's approach should reflect the organization style, meaning a participative style will clash with a rigidly hierarchical organization, and an authoritative style will clash with a participative organization.

ORGANIZATIONAL STRUCTURE

The structure of the organization directly impacts the project efforts. There are a number of organizational structures within the context of project management:

FUNCTIONAL ORGANIZATION

This is a hierarchical organization structure, with staff grouped by specialty. Projects are undertaken from within each group, focused on the function of the group. Communications across functions flow up and back down the functional hierarchy, and project scope is contained within the functional areas. From a project perspective, a functional organization has several disadvantages, including limited span of control, no formal authority for the project manager, team members' focus on their functional assignments versus project work and the difficulty of prioritizing multiple projects. The advantages include grouping of specialists into teams managed by similarly skilled individuals, centralization of similar resources with mutual support through proximity, and clearly defined career paths for functional team members.

The project manager (called project coordinator or project leader) will have little or no authority, acting part-time, and the project team will not be full-time on the project. Any administrative staff will be part time as well.

PROJECTIZED ORGANIZATION

The projectized organization structure is the opposite of a functional organization where team members are often collocated and the majority of the organization's work is project oriented. Project managers have a great deal of independence and authority. Organization units called departments either report directly to the project manager (referred to as a project or program manager), or provide support services to various projects.

Within the project management literature, there are differing views of this structure. The PMBOK Guide perspective is given above.

However, other models labeled "pure projectized" show the functional departments intact, with a separate project team comprised of a project manager with functional department staff assigned exclusively to the project, and the project manager reporting at the same level as the functional managers. The project manager has total authority over the project and may use resources from within or outside the organization.

Disadvantages include duplication of resources and facilities, with the potential for misuse or under-utilization of resources. In addition, as projects are completed, the team members must be reassigned, or released from the organization. When they are reassigned, they may lose their position in the pecking order of the functional unit they came from.

MATRIX ORGANIZATIONS

These types of organizations are designed to highlight the strengths and minimize the weaknesses of functional and projectized organization structures. The matrix organization was designed to manage multiple projects concurrently, while reducing the duplication or resources of a pure projectized organization because team members have "two masters" the project and their ongoing function with their department. The influence of the project manager versus the functional manager will define the type of matrix organization (weak, balanced or strong).

Advantages include improved project manager control versus a functional organization, rapid responses to contingencies (functional or project related), more support from the functional organization, better utilization of scarce resources, coordination of efforts across functional lines, and better balance between time, cost, quality and performance.

The major disadvantage is that project members have a dual reporting structure. In addition, the organization structure is more complex, and may require excess administrative personnel.

WEAK MATRIX ORGANIZATION

This is a hybrid functional organization where staff across functions may work together on a project, one member being appointed as a project coordinator, project leader or project expediter. A project expediter (PE) is a functional position reporting to a departmental manager who has ultimate responsibility for the project. The PE acts as a facilitator, making few decisions, but making recommendations to the departmental manager. They primarily ensure the timely arrival of parts and materials, completion of tasks, and communication of decisions between people and the manager. This delicate balancing act requires unique skills, and this type of structure is typically employed only on small ($10K to $200K) projects. A project coordinator (PC) is a staff position with the ability to assign individuals in the functional organization, and act as a communications channel between upper management and the project team. This, in effect, requires a sharing of authority with the project sponsor. The PC may also perform merit reviews. However, the PC structure leads to higher conflict, again because of the dual reporting requirements of project team members to their functional department head.

BALANCED MATRIX ORGANIZATION

This is a hybrid functional organization where staff across functions may work together on a project, one member being appointed as a full-time project manager or project officer.

STRONG MATRIX ORGANIZATION

This is a hybrid functional organization with an additional group of dedicated project (or program) managers. Project work occurs across organizational functions and is coordinated and managed by project managers from within this group.

COMPOSITE ORGANIZATION

This is similar to a strong matrix organization, but with project coordinators from within the functional areas as well as the dedicated group of project managers.

KEY GENERAL MANAGEMENT SKILLS

General management deals with every aspect of managing an ongoing enterprise and includes finance and accounting, sales and marketing, research and development, manufacturing and distribution; strategic, tactical and operational planning; human resources issues and work relationships and personal time and stress management. Possession of these skills is also essential to a project manager. (It is practically impossible for a project manager to retain the full spectrum of technical skills necessary on a large project, but rather, they should focus on the project management skills required to effectively administer the project.)

There are five key abilities required for being an effective manager:

LEADING

Leading is differentiated from managing in that managing is primarily concerned with consistently producing key results expected by stakeholders while leading involves establishing direction, aligning, motivating, and inspiring people.

COMMUNICATING

The successful transmission or exchange of information is essential so that the recipient understands what the sender intends. This includes verbal, nonverbal, and written communication. A key here is listening as well as communicating, and communications may be external or internal, formal or informal, vertical or horizontal.

NEGOTIATING

This involves conferring with others to reach an agreement. It may involve scope, cost and schedule objectives, or changes to these; contract terms and conditions; assignments and resources.

PROBLEM SOLVING

Problem solving involves a combination of problem definition (distinguishing between causes and symptoms) and decision-making (analyzing problems to determine viable solutions and then making a selection). Note that project decision-making is not limited to project managers. Customers, project team members, functional managers, or other project stakeholders may be involved in decision making.

INFLUENCING THE ORGANIZATION

The ability to get things done is the mark of a great project manager. This requires the ability to identify political realities both inside and outside the organization, as well as having an understanding of the mechanics of power and politics.

Power is the potential ability to influence behavior, change the course of events, and overcome resistance. It is the ability to get people to do something they wouldn't necessarily do. Politics involves getting a collective effort from a group of people with differing interests.

FOUR FUNCTIONS OF THE PROJECT MANAGER

It is widely held that a project manager has these four main functions:

PLANNING

The project manager determines the time, cost, and personnel resources needed to complete the work, which would include team assembly, development of work schedules, and human resource requirements.

ORGANIZING

Assembling the personnel, financial, and physical resources to complete the project.

LEADERSHIP

This is necessary in order to combine resources and administer the project.

CONTROL

Execution of the project plan, and continuous monitoring and measurement of progress as it relates to time, cost and quality.

SOCIOECONOMIC INFLUENCES

In addition to the influences that fall into the category of general management, PMBOK Guide describes the socioeconomic influences that affect projects. The following categories are considered to be key influences with which you should be familiar.

STANDARDS

A document that prescribes a specific consensus solution to a repetitive design, operating, or maintenance problem. Compliance is not mandatory

REGULATION

A regulation is a document that defines product, process, or service characteristics, including the administrative provisions. Compliance is mandatory.

INTERNATIONALIZATION AND CULTURAL INFLUENCES

As organizations achieve global status, and as our world grows ever more interrelated, the project manager must consider the impact of internalization in terms of scope, time, cost, and quality. Time zones, distances, and travel requirements are major elements.

Culture involves the beliefs, behaviors, arts, institutions, and other aspects of a people. Cultural influences include political, economic, demographic, educational, ethical, and religious factors.

PROJECT INTEGRATION MANAGEMENT

The Project Integration Management section on the PMP certification exam addresses critical project management functions that ensure coordination of the various elements of the project. As the PMBOK Guide explains, the processes in integration management are primarily integrative. Project integration management involves making trade-offs among competing objectives in order to meet or exceed stakeholder needs and expectations and addresses project plan development, project plan execution, and overall change control. These three processes not only interact with each other but also interact with processes in the other eight knowledge areas. Noting PMI's view that integration occurs in other areas also is important. For example, project scope and product scope need to be integrated; project work needs to be integrated with the other work of the ongoing organization, and deliverables from various technical specialties need integration.

Prior to the introduction of the new exam format, PMI combined questions on Project Integration Management with those on Project Scope Management. It now addresses these two areas in separate sections. The Project Integration Management questions are straightforward. Most people find them to be easy. Nevertheless, because they cover so much material, you do need to study them carefully to become familiar with PMI's terminology and perspectives. PMBOK Guide figure 4.1 provides an overview of the structure of Project Integration Management.

The Project Integration knowledge area is concerned with coordinating all aspects of the project and is highly interactive. Project planning, project execution, and change control occur throughout the project and are repeated continuously while working on the project. Project planning and execution involve weighing the objectives of the project against alternatives to bring the project to a successful completion. Change control impacts the project plan, which, in turn, impacts execution, so you can see that these three processes are very tightly linked. The processes in this area also interact with other processes in the remaining knowledge areas.

PROJECT DEFINITION

A project is a temporary sequence of tasks with a distinct beginning and an end that is undertaken to create a unique product or service. In addition, a project must have defined objectives in order to clearly indicate when the project has been completed.

There are several attributes that characterize a project:

- **It is directed at achieving a specific result.** Projects have a well-defined set of desired end results. They can be divided into smaller tasks in order to achieve the overall project goal.
- **It involves the coordinated undertaking of interrelated activities.** The various tasks of a project interact with one another, while at the same time interacting with the parent organization.
- **It has a limited duration—a beginning and an end.** Projects progress from an idea through the planning, executing, and controlling steps, and finally to a close. The project life cycle also indicates that the projects are temporary, with a definite beginning and a definite end.
- **It is unique.** The product or service being produced by the project is different and involves doing something that has not been done before.

Progressive elaboration is the essential characteristic of the process by which a project is and should be performed.

NOTE: You should also be familiar with the difference between a project and a program. The term project and program are often used interchangeably. Although these terms are related, they are not the same thing. A program is a group of logically related projects. Frequently, projects are managed together in order to gain benefits that are not available from managing them separately, or because they include similar processes that will benefit from simultaneous management. In addition, programs usually last longer than projects and often have a much less definite end point. Programs may include elements of ongoing operations.

PROJECT MANAGEMENT DEFINITION

Project management includes directing and coordinating various resources throughout the life of a project in order to meet or exceed stakeholder needs, expectations, and requirements. The goal of project management is to achieve the predetermined objectives for scope, quality, time, and cost that have been outlined for a project.

Note that project management is different from managing projects. Managing projects treats many aspects of ongoing operations in an organization as projects, applying project management principles and practices to them.

PROJECT PROCESS GROUPS

The project management process offers clear steps to get projects done on time, within budget, with minimal risks, and with predictable results. In order to begin with a concept and end with a successful product or service, it is critical to complete the five steps below for every project: ("a series of actions bringing about a result").

- **Initiating Processes** - The initiating step involves formally recognizing that a new project exists. Generally, some project goals, objectives, and major milestones are also established during this step.
- **Planning Processes** - This step consists of defining resources and developing a schedule and a budget in order to achieve the project's objectives. This step is generally the most detailed step of the project management process. When done correctly, it has the greatest impact on the success of the project. Since this step is so critical, a common project management phrase to remember is "plan the plan."
- **Executing Processes** - This step involves coordinating people and other resources to carry out the plan. A key phrase to help you remember this step is "work the plan."
- **Controlling Processes** - This step involves ensuring that project objectives are met by monitoring and measuring progress and taking corrective action when necessary.
- **Closing Processes** - The closing step consists of gaining acceptance of the final product, bringing the project to an orderly conclusion, and reviewing lessons learned from the project.

The project management process provides the necessary structure, focus, and organization to successfully complete any project. In order to understand the project management process, you must realize how the five steps of the process work together. Although the initiation step provides a foundation for the rest of the project to build upon and the closing steps helps bring the project to an end, these two steps are not continuous throughout the project management process. They stand on their own at the beginning and the end of the project management process.

The processes are linked as follows:

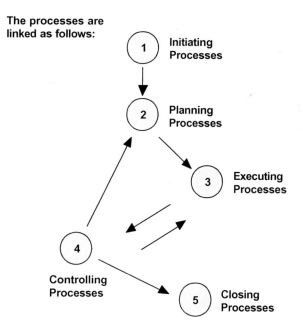

However, the planning, executing, and controlling steps are interdependent and cyclical throughout the entire project. For example, imagine that you have planned to have a ceiling fan in each bedroom in a house that you are building. As you are completing the executing step of building the house, you discover that the contractors did not hang the ceiling fan in the master bedroom. Once you discover this problem, the control step causes you to review all of the related variables to determine why the ceiling fan is missing. For instance, one variable you might want to examine is the communication channel to make sure that the contractors understood the plan. At this point, if you discover the cause of the problem and can still hang the ceiling fan without causing any other problems, you remain in the execution step. However, if hanging the fan causes other problems, you'll examine the project's scope and make changes as necessary.

The figure on the next page depicts the five project management groups and their core and facilitating processes. Please note that the numbers within each component element refer to paragraph citations in *A Guide to the Project Management Body of Knowledge*. PMI expects you to know when certain activities are completed within the chronological framework of these five processes, as well as the inputs, tools and techniques and outputs of each major process. These five project process groups are becoming more and more popular as questions on the PMP exam: initiating processes, planning processes, controlling processes, executing processes, and closing processes. And you need to understand the difference between a core process and a facilitating process. Facilitating processes are those that enable project management; the core processes are involved with the planning and doing of the work itself. They are equally important.

You cannot have a project without both facilitating and core processes, but the key attention goes to the core processes. Make sure you are comfortable with how the flow of those processes go, that there is a need to cycle back from controlling to planning. We do not just plan, execute, control, and close. There are some loops back and forth between controlling and executing, and controlling and planning. And when it comes to closing processes, you need to make sure that you are very comfortable with the difference between contact and administrative closeout.

PROJECT PLAN DEVELOPMENT

The project plan is a key integrative document that uses the outputs of the other planning processes and strategic planning to create a consistent, coherent document that can be used to guide both project execution and project control. Be familiar with what the project plan is used for and what items are often included in a project plan. Also, you should realize that although the project manager is responsible for seeing that the project plan is accomplished, the entire project team must make important contributions to the various pieces of the plan.

NOTE: When it comes to project plan development, what you really need to know is, what, do we use a project plan for? It is used to guide project execution, to document the planning assumption and to document planning decisions regarding some alternatives that have been chosen. We use it to simplify communication between the project team and stakeholders and define key management reviews as to content, expense, and time. It is a baseline for progress management and project control. Is the WBS the project plan? NO. The Work Breakdown Structure is not the project plan—it is a key component of the project plan, but it is not the project plan. Also realize the project schedule is not the project plan. The schedule lists planned dates for performing activities and meeting milestones identified in the project plan.

Although the project manager is responsible for seeing that the project plan is accomplished, all stakeholders, including the entire project team, must make important contributions to the various pieces of the plan. Note also that the project plan is not the performance measurement baseline. The project plan is expected to change throughout the project as more information becomes available,

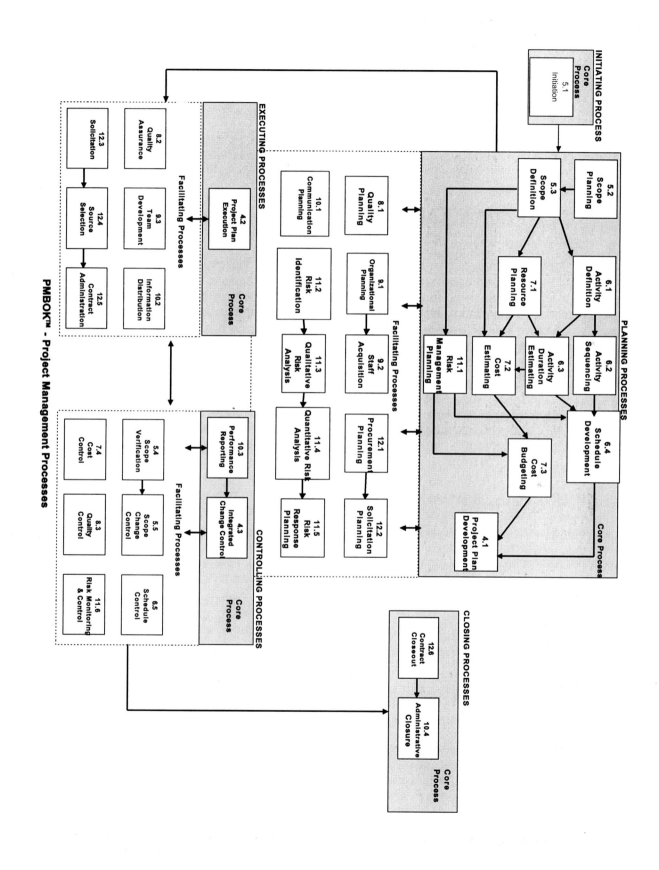

PMBOK™ - Project Management Processes

whereas the performance measurement baselines for technical scope, schedule, and cost are expected to change only intermittently and then, generally, only in response to an approved scope of work or deliverable change. PMI stresses planning as a key success factor in projects.

CONSTRAINTS AND ASSUMPTIONS

Constraints and assumptions are mentioned throughout the PMBOK Guide. Their first mention, though, is in Project Integration Management as an input to project plan development. Constraints are factors that may limit the project management team's options, whereas assumptions are factors that for planning purposes may be considered to be true, real, or certain. Understand the differences between constraints and assumptions, and be able to recognize examples of both. For example, a predefined budget that will limit the team's options is a constraint. The date the project team assumes that a key resource, such as a subject matter expert, may be available to support the project is an assumption.

NOTE: As you work your way through the PMBOK Guide, you will notice that many processes have inputs that include constraints and assumptions. Constraints and assumptions are just that–the constraints of project management and the key assumptions that you make on your project. It allows latitude for every organization to have a different interpretation of what a project is. Specifically, however, you should be most aware of the triple constraint, and that triple constraint is time, cost, and requirements.

PROJECT PLANNING METHODOLOGY

Be familiar with the use and purpose of a project planning methodology, that is, any structured approach to help prepare the project plan. It may be simple, consisting of forms and templates. Or it may be complex, such as required simulations to perform schedule or cost risk analysis. PMI makes the distinction between "hard" tools in a methodology, such as project management software, and "soft" tools, such as a facilitated kickoff meeting.

NOTE: When it comes to project planning, the key issue you need to understand here is that organizations should have some kind of methodology that they follow as to project planning, something that lends a little consistency to the processes they are using internally. This process should be a good blend of hard and soft tools. Make sure you have that distinction down as well.

STAKEHOLDER KNOWLEDGE AND SKILLS

Project stakeholders are individuals and organizations that are actively involved in a project or whose interests may be affected by project execution and completion. Stakeholders also may exert influence over the project and its results. Key stakeholders on every project include such persons as the project manager, customer, performing organization, team members, and sponsor. Recognize the importance of involving stakeholders in the development of the project plan. One key objective of stakeholder management is to minimize the effect of the actions of stakeholders who are against the project.

NOTE: You are working on a project. A key element of that project is to make sure that your deliverables absolutely, positively get there overnight. Suddenly, in a project where, it has nothing to do with the capability to deliver, as a carrier would deliver, the carrier becomes a key stakeholder. It becomes vital for you to know whether the carrier you have selected has the expertise to enable you to complete your project as the customer anticipates. That is what PMI is striving for here. It is looking at the importance of making sure all stakeholders are identified and that their roles in the process are identified as well.

PROJECT MANAGEMENT INFORMATION SYSTEM (PMIS)

Note that the PMIS is a tool used by each of the three project integration management processes used to gather, integrate, and distribute the outputs of other project management processes. It is simply an information system that stores all of the information related to your project. The PMIS is used from the beginning of the project through closeout. It may be software such as Microsoft Project, Microsoft Access or it may be a manual system.

NOTE: Knowing what it is, is key. There will be several questions about the project management information system on the exam. They are not just looking for software tools. Tools such as computer software may be used as part of the information system, but the system is not exclusively made up of those components. It is made up of software, forms, templates, memos, and the processes that go into funneling information through your project.

EARNED VALUE MANAGEMENT (EVM)

EVM is mentioned throughout the PMBOK Guide but its first mention is as a tool and technique for project plan development. EVM is used to integrate the project's scope, schedule, and resources and to measure and report project performance, from initiation to closeout. More information is provided on EVM in the Project Cost Management Chapter. The exam contains many EVM questions so make sure you have a thorough understanding of EVM.

PROJECT PLAN EXECUTION

Project plan execution is defined as the process during which the project plan is carried out, the majority of the project's budget is spent, and the project manager and team members spend the majority of their time. Accordingly, performance against the baseline must be continuously monitored.

NOTE: As one of the key project management processes, this one will have the inputs, tools and techniques, and the outputs listed in the PMBOK Guide. As you read the PMBOK Guide, take special note of what the inputs are versus the outputs. In many cases on the PMP exam, what is asked is which of the following is not an input to the process. Three choices will be inputs and one will be an output, which happens to be an output from the very same process. You should know what the inputs and what the outputs are to any given process.

ORGANIZATIONAL POLICIES AND PROCEDURES

The PMBOK Guide considers organizational policies as an input to both project plan development and project plan execution. These policies are both formal and informal and involve any and all organizations involved in the project. Organizational procedures are included as tools and techniques of project plan execution. Specifically, organizational policies include such things as quality management, personnel administration, and the financial controls that are in place.

CORRECTIVE AND PREVENTIVE ACTION

Corrective action appears throughout the PMBOK Guide. It is first introduced in Project Integration Management as an input to project plan execution. Corrective action is defined as anything done to bring expected future performance in line with the plan. In short, corrective action is the day-to-day responses to all the obstacles and problems a project may encounter. Preventive action is anything that reduces the probability of potential consequences of potential risk events.

NOTE: The description of corrective action: it is what is important about it when it comes to integration management. Specifically, this is the one and only spot that it is an input into the process. Throughout the rest of the PMBOK Guide, it is an output.

MANAGEMENT BY OBJECTIVES (MBO)

Another area that often appears on one or more versions of the test and that is not covered specifically in the PMBOK Guide is MBO. This managerial leadership system defines individual managerial responsibilities in terms of corporate objectives. It has been described as a technique for promoting better plans and performance. The project manager interfaces with MBO in a number of ways depending on whether it is implemented (1) by the organization's top management; (2) by the project manager; or (3) by and in a separate functional department. MBO works best when it is implemented and fully supported by top management. The project's and the project manager's goals and objectives should reflect corporate and top management goals, as well as the customer's or client's goals.

The most important use of MBO is with subsystems and individual parts of the project. Preparing the work breakdown structure (WBS) is the best place to start, because it results in the project being broken down into readily accomplishable subdivisions.

MBO is a three-step process:

1. Establish unambiguous and realistic objectives.
2. Periodically evaluate whether project objectives are being achieved.

3. Act upon the results of the evaluation.

Good objectives are unambiguously stated and contain a measure of how to assess whether they have been achieved. To be realistic, objectives must be determined jointly by managers and those who are to perform the work-a top-down, bottom-up process.

NOTE: For this section, one thing you should know is Peter Drucker is responsible for management by objectives. You should also know that MBO is a concept that should be supported by management. MBO also comes with unambiguous objectives, realistic objectives, mutually accepted objectives, and measurable objectives. Measurability is key when it comes to MBO.

WORK AUTHORIZATION SYSTEM

A work authorization system is another tool for project plan execution. It is authorization to begin work on a specific activity or work package. Although most work is authorized in writing, verbal authorizations are common on smaller projects. The basic notion advanced by PMI is that work cannot commence without the appropriate person's authorization.

NOTE: "Neal, go program something!" That is a classic work authorization system. Often a work system is authorized and implemented verbally. We do not necessarily have to have some kind of formal, written documentation to back up the work authorization system. What you need to know is that verbal authorization is a tool associated with project plan execution, and it is something that made, ideally, in writing.

PROJECT EVALUATION

Evaluation is one method by which project managers can check on how their projects are progressing. There are two major types of evaluation and each has a specific purpose.

MID-PROJECT EVALUATION

Conducted while the project is still under way, the purpose of mid-project evaluation is to determine whether the project is meeting its objectives and to reassess whether the objectives are still relevant and worthwhile. People outside the project team who have the necessary experience and/or skills often conduct a mid-project evaluation so that the results are more objective and less biased.

Potential outcomes of a mid-project evaluation include the following:

- Identification of significant problems and the need for specific changes.
- Significant changes in the project's objectives.
- Termination of the project.

Potential problems that can plague mid-project evaluation efforts include the following:

- Some senior managers may misuse an evaluation to identify and punish poor performers.
- Some senior managers may misuse an evaluation to accomplish or support political agendas.
- Project teams often resist evaluation (do not cooperate with the process) because of the possible negative outcomes and because they are often evaluated by outsiders.
- Evaluation can be disruptive because it takes time to prepare for, conduct, and review the results of the evaluation.
- Project teams being evaluated worry that the process will be carried out in an arbitrary and inconsistent fashion, possibly making the evaluation results misleading or invalid.

FINAL OR POSTPROJECT EVALUATION

A final or post project evaluation is conducted after the project has been completed. The purpose is to identify lessons learned so that they can be shared with other project teams.

NOTE: There is much information in this section but what you need to know is the difference between evaluation, monitoring, and control. Monitoring and control are the small, incremental steps that are taken on daily—for example, stopping by and asking how someone is doing. Evaluation is the large-scale information that we go out to gather. It normally costs money to gather that kind of information, and it usually takes time.

CUSTOMER SATISFACTION

Customer satisfaction is most closely related to the idea of a careful and accurate needs analysis so that customer or stakeholder expectations can be identified and then satisfied. Pay careful attention to what PMI says about customers/stakeholders, managing expectations, and needs analysis. The project management team's responsibility is to identify the stakeholders, determine their requirements, and manage the process to ensure a successful project. PMI notes that it is difficult to identify stakeholders and that managing their expectations also is difficult because often stakeholders have conflicting or contradictory objectives. The project management team must find appropriate resolutions to such differences.

NOTE: There a couple of key aspects associated with customer satisfaction—one is stakeholders. You need to identify all the stakeholders in a project and identify all their needs. Another aspect associated with customer satisfaction is meeting the scope. If we meet the scope of the project as requested by the customer, then we should have complete customer satisfaction.

PROGRESS REPORTS

You should be familiar with why it is important to measure progress and with some of the common progress reporting techniques.

REASONS FOR MEASURING PROGRESS

- To determine whether the project is on target, that is, to compare actual performance to the project plan.
- To identify problems and issues so that corrective action can be taken.

COMMON PROGRESS REPORTING TECHNIQUES

- Status reports
- Progress reports
- Forecasts
- Trend analysis
- Variance analysis
- Exception reports
- Status review meetings
- Earned value reports
- Schedule reporting (examples - Gantt charts, Milestone charts, Network diagrams)
- Cost reporting (examples - Expenditure tables, Histograms, S-curves)

NOTE: When it comes to progress reports, one thing that may trip you up is the difference between a progress report, a status report, and a forecast. A progress report is a look at the project. What progress have we made to date? What things have we accomplished? A status report asks: Where are we today? What have we done to date? A forecast, on the other hand, looks at where are we going to be in the future.

WORK RESULTS

Work results are outputs of project plan execution. They are the activities performed to accomplish the project. Information on the status of work results is collected as part of the project's reporting process.

NOTE: Work results are an output of the project plan execution process. Specifically, they are the deliverables. They are what we have produced for our efforts.

CHANGE REQUESTS

Another output of project plan execution is change requests. As ideas for change come in from all stakeholders, a designated team member records all change requests in a change log, noting their source, the date, and a description of the change. Each change request will have a unique identifier, usually a number, so that it can be tracked and referenced. Examples, as provided in the PMBOK Guide, include a request to expand or contract project scope, or modify cost or schedule estimates. This leads to the third process in Project Integration Management, integrated change control.

NOTE: This is another area cross-referenced throughout the PMBOK Guide. What is important to take away from this section is when it comes to change requests, change control, or any issue associated with changes, document everything.

INTEGRATED CHANGE CONTROL

The purpose of integrated change control is to influence factors that create change so that the change is beneficial, determine when a change has occurred, and manage actual changes if and when they do occur. This process is concerned with coordinating changes across the entire project as shown in PMBOK Guide figure 4.2.

CHANGE CONTROL SYSTEM

The change control system is the principal tool used for integrated change control. As described in PMBOK Guide, it consists of formal, documented procedures that define the steps used to change formal documents.

A well-developed and documented change control process is crucial to the project management process success. The basic objectives of a change control system are to:

- Continually identify changes, actual or proposed, as they occur.
- Reveal the consequences of the proposed changes in terms of cost and schedule impacts.
- Permit managerial analysis, investigation of alternatives, and an acceptance or rejection checkpoint.
- Communicate changes to all stakeholders.
- Insure that approved changes are implemented.
- Update the development process.

NOTE: Some organizations assign the project manager a level of authority for accepting change requests. This does not mean that the project manager can arbitrarily make the changes. It means the he can make recommendations for changes to the customer without first consulting management, provided the request is for a change that does not affect the budget or schedule more than a preset amount. Otherwise, the change requests are passed through the project manager to a change control board (CCB) for review.

CHANGE CONTROL BOARD (CCB)

The CCB may be part of a change control system and be responsible for approving or rejecting change requests. Although some projects may have multiple CCBs, there are circumstances under which the project manager may be able to handle certain types of changes without the need for a formal CCB review.

NOTE: A change control system consists of a formal, documented procedure for handling change. However, you do need to be aware that a change control board, or a CCB, is what is responsible for authorizing the change that goes through this system.

CONFIGURATION MANAGEMENT

The basic thrust of configuration management is to do the following:

- Carefully define a system deliverable.
- Rigorously control changes to the deliverable.
- Ensure that the ultimate deliverable is consistent with the defined system as modified by approved changes.

The purpose of the configuration management approach is to establish a contractual orientation. Make sure you do exactly what you said you would do and comply with the end user's stated desires. Configuration management protects the end user from unauthorized changes by project staff and protects the project staff from shifts in the end user's desires.

BASIC STEPS IN CONFIGURATION MANAGEMENT

- **Develop the specifications** - Develop the specifications for a complete program configuration item (CPCI). Have the end user sign off on these specifications.
- **Develop a general design** - Develop the general design of a CPCI directly from the specifications describing the deliverable and nothing else. Thus the specifications serve as the baseline for the general design. There should be a one-to-one relationship between specification items and items in the general design. Inspect the specifications and general design to ensure that they are compatible.
- **Develop a detailed design** - Repeat the process above, except this time use the general design as the baseline for the detailed design. Inspect the detailed design for compatibility with the general design.
- **Implement and test the system** - Use the detailed design as the guide to carrying out the project. Rigorously control changes to the design. In testing the system, compare system performance against the original specifications (as modified through a controlled approval process). Remember that the original specification is the only document in which the user agreed upon a description of what the system is supposed to do.

- **Audit the items and system to verify conformance to requirements** - An audit should be conducted to ensure that what has been designed conforms to the specific requirements. These audits may be called functional configuration audits or physical configuration audits.

CHANGE CONTROL IN CONFIGURATION MANAGEMENT

The three basic objectives of a change control are:

1. Screen the user requests
   - Use a request for change form.
   - Assess the consequences of the requested changes.
   - If the request has no effect on the project it objectives, it can be accepted by the project manager. Otherwise, it should be approved by a higher level of management.
2. Keep track of accepted changes. Keep a file of accepted changes and always update specifications based on changes.
3. Update the development process. Update all baselines and inform project staff of changes.

NOTE: The basic steps are outlines here, and what you need to understand is that these steps lead you to a notion called traceability. You can trace the general design, to the detailed design, back to the general design, and back to the specifications. Also understand that in configuration management change control, there is ardent screening going on. All changes must be screened, tracked, accepted, approved, and the development process updated.

LESSONS LEARNED

Lessons learned are mentioned throughout the PMBOK Guide but are first addressed in Project Integration Management as an output of integrated change control. PMBOK Guide paragraph 4.3.3.3 states that lessons learned need to be documented to show the causes of variances and the reasons for selecting the corrective actions. This information is to be available for use on the current project and for other projects in the organization. Documenting lessons learned also is an important practice because it relates to the area of professional responsibility.

NOTE: This is not the last time you are going to see this output. It is an output of many project management processes. What is important about lessons learned is to recognize that they are an inherent part of every project and every process. They are also crucial not only to the project team but to the performing organization as a whole.

CHAPTER REVIEW

1. Which of the following is a tool or technique used in project plan execution to exchange information about the project?
   A. Status review meeting
   B. General management skills
   C. Organizational procedures
   D. Work-authorization system

2. You are working on a top secret satellite project for the government. The product plan and system requirements have been determined and agreed to by senior military officials and all other stakeholders. Work is proceeding on the project according to schedule. Everyone seems pleased with the progress to date. You have just learned that a new regulatory requirement will cause a change in one of the project's performance specifications. To ensure that this change is incorporated into the project plan, you should:
   A. Update the work breakdown structure
   B. Call a meeting of the change control board
   C. Immediately inform all stakeholders and wait for a go ahead
   D. Prepare a change request

3. _____ is a formal, approved document used to manage and control project execution.
   A. Project plan
   B. Organizational policies
   C. Organizational procedures
   D. Work authorization system

4. You have just been hired as a project manger and have been given your first project. You are not sure where to start on project planning so you decided to rely on which of the following to help you plan your project?
   A. Historical information
   B. Staff management plan
   C. Resource assignment matrix
   D. Project management training

5. As project manager, you recently submitted a product plan that was approved by all stakeholders. Work is proceeding on the project according to schedule. Everyone seems pleased with the progress to date. You have just learned that the client needs to make a major scope change to comply with a new regulatory requirement going into effect. To ensure that this change is incorporated into the project plan, you should:
   A. Update the work breakdown structure
   B. Immediately inform all stakeholders and wait for a go ahead
   C. Prepare a change request
   D. Call a meeting of the change control board

6. You are the project manager for a large nuclear construction project with a team of eight highly skilled staff members. Several team members like to do tasks when they want to, regardless of the order in which these tasks appear in a project schedule. You are concerned that this informal method of task completion will be detrimental to the project. With your concern looming overhead you decide to call a team meeting to discuss which procedures to implement to ensure that work is done at the right time and in the right sequence. At this meeting, you put into place a:
   A. Resource management plan
   B. Work authorization system
   C. Change control system
   D. Resource authorization matrix

7. You are a project manager for a leading software development company and you are working on a project that will compete with the current popular word processing program, by providing, e-mail, spreadsheet and word processing from one application. Your project sponsor asked you to describe the total product scope of this project. You told him it is the:
   A. WBS and project activity list
   B. Project requirements that have been approved by stakeholders
   C. Work packages that comprise the non-project management elements in the WBS
   D. Sum of the integrated management control plans

8. _____ is a document or collection of documents that should be expected to change over time as more information becomes available about the project.
   A. Additional work authorizations
   B. Project monitoring plan
   C. Change request
   D. Project plan

9. As project manager for a major pharmaceutical company you have come to realize the importance of status review meetings. You also know from experience that your project team and stakeholders usually do not want to attend these meetings. You are now entering the final phase of clinical trials for what you hope is a cure for rheumatoid arthritis. Because you are in the final project execution phase, these meetings:
   A. Can be reduced in frequency
   B. Should be held frequently
   C. Should be conducted weekly with project sponsors only
   D. Must be scheduled regularly document general project goals

10. Which of the following is a tool or technique used in integrated change control to assess whether variances from the plan require corrective action?
   A. Performance reports
   B. Performance measurement
   C. Project plan updates
   D. Organizational procedures

11. You are managing a large project with twenty stakeholders in three continents. Sixteen different contractors are involved and all their work must be coordinated. With a project this size in scope you realize that you must devote a lot of attention to effective integrated change control. This means you are concerned primarily with:
    A. Establishing a change control board that oversees the overall project changes
    B. Influencing factors that cause change, determining that change has occurred, and managing actual changes as they occur
    C. Integrating deliverables from different functional specialties on the project
    D. Maintaining baseline integrity, integrating product and project scope, and coordinating change across knowledge areas

12. Your project has several different work results. You and your team have spent several days gathering information about these work results, such as what costs have been incurred, which deliverables have been completed, and which remain outstanding. You will use this information in which of the following processes?
    A. Performance review
    B. Scope verification
    C. Integrated change control
    D. Project plan development

13. Outputs of change control include all of the following except:
    A. Project plan updates
    B. Corrective action
    C. Lessons learned
    D. Work breakdown structure updates

14. The project planning methodology is defined in the PMBOK Guide as:
    A. Using planning techniques to achieve a desired end goal
    B. A structured approach used to guide a team during development of a project plan
    C. Organizational policies
    D. General management skills

15. According to PMI, the project plan is primarily used to?
    A. Develop corrective measures
    B. Help prevent scope changes
    C. Facilitate communication between stakeholders
    D. Finalize budget cost estimates

16. According to PMI, which of the following is a collection of formal, documented procedures that defines how project performance will be monitored and evaluated?
    A. Lessons learned
    B. Concurrent engineering
    C. Change control system
    D. Project charter

17. You have just finished reading the PMBOK Guide and realize that historical information is used:
    A. During project risk analysis only
    B. Throughout the project management process
    C. Only if a risk identified
    D. To help with risk identification

18. You remember reading in the PMBOK Guide that project planning methodologies are structured approaches to guide the project team as it develops the project plan. You have decided to develop a project planning methodology for your company, and you want to include in it both "hard" and "soft" tools. Which one of the following is an example of a "soft" tool?
    A. Project management information storage systems
    B. Project management information systems
    C. A facilitated kickoff meeting
    D. Budgetary accounting codes

19. You are the project manager for a new systems project dealing with aircraft cargo holds. Management of course wants your project to yield a high-value but at a low cost. You have been reading several documents and realize that you would like to take the time and money to incorporate features that would increase long-term project value, but one of your major vendors employs senior-level staff that typically cost more than other vendors charge. When working with stakeholders, you should:
    A. Group stakeholders into categories for easy identification
    B. Be sensitive to the fact that stakeholders often have very different objectives and that this makes stakeholder management difficult
    C. Recognize that roles and responsibilities may overlap
    D. Curtail stakeholder activities that might have a negative effect on the project

20. A technique that is used to integrate the project's scope, schedule, and resources, as well as to measure and report project performance from initiation to closeout is known as?
    A. Earned value management
    B. Project management information system
    C. Value added management
    D. Change control

ANSWERS

1. A
2. D
3. A
4. A
5. C
6. B
7. D
8. D
9. A
10. B
11. B
12. A
13. D
14. B
15. C
16. C
17. B
18. C
19. B
20. A

PROJECT SCOPE MANAGEMENT

Scope management focuses on identifying and controlling the work that is required to complete a project. This action results in a product with well-defined features and functions. In order to manage the scope of a project successfully, you must understand the following components of scope management:

- Project initiation – consists of recognizing that there is a new project.
- Scope planning – includes writing a scope statement.
- Scope definition and verification - consists of breaking project deliverables into small pieces and formalizing acceptance of the project scope.
- Scope change control, includes identifying and managing changes to the project scope.

The Project Scope Management questions on the PMP exam cover a diverse, yet functional set of project management topics: project planning, work breakdown structures, project life cycles, project charter, project selection methods, scope statement, scope verification, scope management plan, and the scope changes are among the topics covered.

PMI views project scope management as a five-step process that consists of initiation, scope planning, scope definition, scope verification, and scope change control. In the PMBOK Guide figure 5.1 provides an overview of the structure.

The project scope management questions on the exam are straightforward. Most people have found them to be easy; do not be lulled into a full sense of security by past results. These questions cover a wide range of material, and you must be familiar with the terminology and perspectives adopted by PMI.

Project Scope Management has five processes: Initiation, Scope Planning, Scope Definition, Scope Verification, and Scope Change Control.

Project Scope Management is concerned with the work of the project. All of the processes involved with the work of the project, and only the work that is required to complete the project are found in this knowledge area. Scope Planning, Scope Definition, Scope Verification, and Scope Change Control involve detailing the requirements of the project and the activities that will eventually comprise the project plan, verifying those details using measurements techniques, and controlling changes to these processes.

PROJECT LIFE CYCLE

Numerous questions may appear on the test relating to the project life cycle. PMI states that the project life cycle defines the beginning and end of the project, describes the technical work to be done in each phase, and identifies who should be involved. Life-cycle descriptions may be general or detailed with the more detailed approaches often called project management methodologies. Most life-cycle descriptions share these common characteristics:

- Cost and staffing levels are minimal at the start of the project, increase toward the end, and then drop off when the project comes to an end.
- The probability of successfully completing the project is low at the start because uncertainty is high. The probability of successful completion gets progressively higher as the project continues and work is completed. Therefore, there is always a higher degree of risk at the beginning of any project.
- The ability of stakeholders to influence the final characteristics of the project's product and final cost is highest at the start and then gets progressively lower as the project continues. This is because the cost of changes and error correction increases geometrically as the project nears completion. This fact underscores the importance of gathering accurate requirements at the beginning of a project.

Know the four phases of the life cycle and be able to identify activities associated with each life-cycle phase. PMI recognizes a variety of possible project life cycles. However, the life cycle tested on the exam usually consists of the following four phases and associated activities:

CONCEPT PHASE
- Gather data
- Identify needs and alternatives
- Establish goals, feasibility, risk, and strategy
- Guesstimate resources
- Present proposal
- Develop project charter

NOTE: What you need to take away from the concept phase is that this is the earliest stage of a project.

DEVELOPMENT (PLANNING) PHASE

- Appoint project manager and key team members
- Develop performance measurement baseline
- Establish master plan, budget, work breakdown structure, and policies/procedures
- Assess risks
- Confirm justification and obtain approval to proceed

NOTE: The development phase is still early in the process. It is the phase where we draft the budget, the schedule, and the project plan. It is also when we make the first comprehensive draft of the work breakdown structure. We finalize the plan here and make the final commitment to do the work for the project.

IMPLEMENTATION (EXECUTION) PHASE

- Set up organization
- Establish detailed technical requirements
- Set up and execute work packages
- Direct, monitor, and control scope, quality, time, cost, and risks

NOTE: In the implementation phase, we perform and do the work as prescribed in the WBS.

TERMINATION/CLOSEOUT (FINISHING) PHASE

- Review and accept project
- Receive formal acceptance
- Transfer responsibility, document and evaluate results
- Release and redirect resources

NOTE: We often overlook the termination phase. It is the most underrated of the phases. It is where we do both contract closeout and administrative closeout. A critical component here is lessons learned.

INITIATION

It is important to understand that the project initiation not only is a component of the project scope variable, but also constitutes the first step in the project management process–project initiating.

Project initiation occurs when an individual or group recognizes that a project should begin. Although project initiation is not always a clearly defined process, it frequently includes determining what the project should accomplish, defining the goal of project, and developing a project charter. These actions might vary depending on the organization for which the project is done.

PMI defines initiation as the process that formally recognizes the beginning of a new project or the continuation of an existing project into its next phase. Note that projects are authorized in different ways in different organizations. PMBOK Guide section 5.1 lists typical reasons to authorize projects, including market demand, business needs, customer request, technological advance, or social need.

Inputs to initiation consist of: product description, strategic plan, project selection criteria, and historical information

The PMBOK Guide notes the importance of relating the product description to the business need or other stimuli that gave rise to the product. The PMBOK Guide states that the product description will generally have fewer details in early phases and more details in later phases as the product characteristics are progressively elaborated. The PMBOK Guide also notes the need for projects to support an organization's strategic plan. In the initiation process, the PMBOK Guide identifies the identification and assignment of the project manager as a key output and suggests that the project manager be assigned as early as possible in the project but always before project plan execution begins.

NOTE: Initiation is where we get our work. This is a concept that is important, since it is where the project manager is assigned and where he/she can point to the beginning of the project. This is challenging, since many projects might be born out of thin air and do not often have a clear beginning point.

PROJECT SELECTION TECHNIQUES
Be familiar with common project selection techniques, which involve measuring value to the project owner. Techniques include considering the decision criterion and calculating value under uncertainty—the decision method and the calculation method. Project selection also applies to choosing alternative ways to complete the project. Two categories of selection techniques are identified:

- Benefit Measurement Methods
- Constrained Optimization Methods

BENEFIT MEASUREMENT METHODS
- Comparative approaches
- Benefit contribution
- Scoring models
- Economic models

The following are specific examples of benefit measurement methods that may appear on the exam.

PRESENT VALUE

Present value is defined as the value in current monetary units of work to be performed in the future. It is determined by discounting the future price of work by a rate (discount rate) commensurate with the interest rate on the funds for the period before payment is required. In simple terms, present value is the value today of future cash flows.

For a given future payment t years from now

$$PV = Mt/(1 + r)^t$$

$M_{t\,=\,amount}$ of payment t years from now

r = interest rate (sometimes called "discount rate")

t = time period

NET PRESENT VALUE

Net present value (NPV) is the present value of all the revenues less the present value of all the goods. A positive result indicates that the revenues are greater than the costs and, therefore, the project is worth pursuing. A negative result is the opposite and indicates the project is a losing proposition. A zero result shows that the project will break even.

NOTE: Although we have observed a decrease in the number of present value questions on the exam, you should be knowledgeable of the concept.

BENEFIT-COST RATIO (BCR)

Benefit-cost analysis results in the calculation of a benefit-cost ratio. This provides a measure of the expected profitability of a project by dividing expected revenues by expected costs. Although some managers prefer relatively simple and straightforward measures of benefits and costs, in practice, the measures of the benefits and the costs are sometimes modified to consider more complex trade-offs. However, the exam does not test the exact formulas, focusing instead on the concept. You should know the following:

- A BCR of 1.0 means that expected benefits and costs are equal, that is, you have a break-even project.
- A BCR less than 1.0 means that costs are expected to exceed benefits, that is, the project is not financially attractive.
- A BCR greater than 1.0 is a profitable project. The higher the ratio, the more profitable the project. For example, a BCR of 2.5 means that you expect a gross payback of $2.50 for every dollar expended on the project.

INTERNAL RATE OF RETURN (IRR)

IRR is another quantitative measure of a project's expected profitability. IRR can be thought of as the average rate of return for the project, measured as a percentage. In other words, the IRR is the interest rate that makes the present value of costs equal to the present value of benefits. Therefore, an IRR of 0.22 means that you expect the project to return an average of 0.22 percent per time period (usually measured in years). The higher the IRR, the better the project's return to the organization.

PAYBACK PERIOD

The payback period is defined as the number of time periods up to the point where cumulative revenues exceed cumulative costs, and therefore the project has finally "turned a profit." When comparing two or more projects, the shortest payback period identifies the project that becomes profitable most quickly. However, the payback period does not identify the expected magnitude of the total profit.

OPPORTUNITY COST

Opportunity cost is the cost of choosing one alternative and, therefore, giving up the potential benefits of another alternative. The understanding of opportunity cost causes management to treat project selection seriously because the organization is committing valuable, finite resources through decisions that often cannot be changed easily in the short run. Poor project selection may cause the company to miss out on better opportunities.

SUNK COST

Sunk costs are expended costs over which we no longer have control; they are "water under the bridge." Because the money is already spent many financial analysts have long professed that sunk costs should be ignored when making decisions about whether to continue investing in a project that is under way.

CONSTRAINED OPTIMIZATION METHODS

These methods include a variety of mathematical programming models that are used less often than other methods because they are more difficult to understand and use. Several examples follow.

- Linear and nonlinear programming
- Integer programming
- Dynamic programming
- Multiobjective programming
- Decision trees
- Forced choice
- Analytic hierarchy process
- Logical framework analysis

As a result, when organizations apply complex project selection criteria in a sophisticated model, it may be beneficial to treat the use of this model as a separate project phase.

NOTE: It is not likely that you will encounter more than a question or two on this topic. Occasionally they will ask you to actually select which is the better project. More commonly, the question will evolve around, which one means which thing? In other words, what is a peer review? What is a murder board? A murder board, by the way, is similar to a college review, where you stand before a board and try to defend its usefulness.

You need to know the various benefit-cost models. Understand the difference between a benefit-cost ratio (benefits first, then cost), and a cost-benefit ratio (cost first, and then benefits).

For the constrained optimization method, all you simply need to know the terms and that they are mathematical programming models.

EXPERT JUDGMENT

Expert judgment is mentioned throughout the PMBOK Guide but is first discussed as a tool and technique in the initiation process. Any group or individual with specialized knowledge applicable to the specific project may provide expertise—people in other units within the performing organization, outside consultants, stakeholders (including customers), professional and technical associations, and industry groups.

PROJECT DELIVERABLES

Project deliverables identify what the project is supposed to produce. For example, the purpose of a project might be to create a new service or to fix a current product defect. The term deliverables is used too frequently in project management because the focus is on the outputs. Focusing on outputs helps define the boundaries of the project and keeps the team focused on the project goal.

It is important to realize that there are both intermediate and end deliverables. An end deliverable is the final product of the project. For example, a document that identified the technical specifications for a new software program is an intermediate deliverable, while the actual software program is considered the end deliverable. In order to clearly show how the work of the project will actually be completed, all deliverables should be defined in terms of a tangible, verifiable product or service.

PROJECT CHARTER

You should know what a project charter is and what it does for the project manager. The project charter officially does the following:

- Establishes the project.
- Authorizes the project manager to use organizational resources to accomplish project activities.
- Provides a general description of project objectives.

You should also know that the charter should be created during the concept phase of a project, and it is normally created by upper management. The project manager may or may not be personally involved in creating the project charter (this practice varies among companies). It is a key output of the initiating process of Project Scope Management and normally is issued by a manager external to the project at a level in the organization appropriate to the needs of the project. Without a charter, it is difficult for the project manager to operate with the level of authority required, especially in a matrix environment.

NOTE: This is a document that has gained much importantance and significance over the last few years; thus, you can expect at least a couple questions about it. It does establish the project and is only valid if it is signed. There needs to be a signature on a project charter. Know that it also establishes the authority for the project manager.

SCOPE PLANNING

Scope planning is the process during which the scope statement is prepared. The scope statement is important because it serves as the basis for future project decisions and includes the criteria to determine whether the entire project or a particular phase of the project has been completed successfully. Furthermore, the scope statement forms the basis for an agreement between the project team and the customer by identifying the project objectives and deliverables.

Tools and techniques for scope planning include product analysis and benefit/cost analysis (see earlier discussion of benefit-cost ratio under benefit measurement methods). Product analysis is used to develop a better understanding of the project's product. You should be familiar with some of the product analysis techniques:

PRODUCT BREAKDOWN ANALYSIS ENGINEERING

Involves developing a better understanding of the product by breaking it down into constituent parts.

VALUE ENGINEERING

Examines each element of a product or system to determine whether there is a more effective and less expensive way to achieve the same function.

VALUE ANALYSIS

Focuses on optimizing cost performance. Systematic use of techniques to identify the required functions of an item, establish values for those functions, and provide the functions at the lowest overall cost without loss of performance.

FUNCTION ANALYSIS

Examines the project's high-level requirements statements, identifying specific functions and estimating total costs based on the number of functions to be performed.

QUALITY FUNCTION DEPLOYMENT (QFD)

A customer-driven planning tool that guides the design, manufacturing, and marketing of goods. Every decision is made to meet the expressed needs of customers. A set of matrices is developed to relate the voice of the customer to the product's technical requirements, component requirements, process control plans, and manufacturing operations. These matrices comprise the House of Quality. The House of Quality is the first matrix in a four-phase QFD process. It's called the House of Quality because of the correlation matrix that is roof shaped and sits on top of the main body of the matrix. The correlation matrix evaluates how the defined product specifications optimize or sub-optimize each other.

The PMBOK Guide strongly recommends a written scope statement even if its elements have been included in other documents, such as the project charter. Elements that comprise the scope statement (project justification, project product, project deliverables, and project objectives) are discussed in the PMBOK Guide.

The PMBOK Guide, also recommends that a scope management plan be prepared. The scope management plan should include a clear description of how scope changes will be identified and classified. This is particularly difficult, but it is absolutely essential when the product characteristics are still being elaborated. This may be a stand-alone document, or it may be part of the project plan.

NOTE: If we have a good statement of work, do we need a scope statement? The answer is yes. We have a detailed project requirements document, do we need a scope statement? The answer is yes.

When don't we need a scope statement? The short answer is virtually never. PMI is very big on the scope statement. It is a foundation document. It is a major component of the way business is done. It clarifies and guides; it is fundamental.

SCOPE DEFINITION

Scope definition is the process of breaking all of the major project deliverables into smaller elements. This process should be completed for each of the project deliverables listed in the scope statement.

It is important to understand that scope definition is a component of the project scope variable and that it is also part of the second step in the project management process–planning.

NOTE: Defining the scope–breaking down the work so that you can clearly understand all the work that has to be done. If you understand that, you know what you need to know about scope definition.

WORK BREAKDOWN STRUCTURE (WBS)

If you were to take a car trip to a town less than 100 miles away, you may not need to do a lot of planning. Just hop in the car and go. However, if you were driving from New York City to Miami and then Los Angeles, you would most likely spend some time looking at maps and researching your route. Somehow, you would break the big trip down into smaller pieces, like miles per day or geographic borders such as states. Nevertheless, whatever approach you use, the only way to accurately plan a trip of this size is to break it down into smaller parts

The same is true for projects. You may understand a project well enough to balance its cost-schedule-quality equilibrium, but you also need to be able to break it down–to understand the whole project by understanding it parts. The work breakdown structure (WBS) is the tool for breaking down a project into component parts. It is the foundation of project planning and one of the most important techniques used in project management. If done well, it can become the secret to successful project management.

The work breakdown structure identifies all the tasks in a project; in fact, a WBS is sometimes referred to simply as a task list. It turns one large, unique project, into many small manageable tasks. The WBS uses outputs from project definition and risk management and identifies the tasks that are the foundation for all subsequent planning.

A WBS is a technique for breaking down a project into its component elements. It is a graphic picture of the hierarchy of the project, broken down level by level into subprojects and finally into tasks. It organizes the project by defining all the tasks that must be performed in the conception, design, development, fabrication, and test of the project hardware, software, or service. As the levels become lower, the scope, complexity, and cost of each subproject become smaller, until the tasks that are completely capable of accomplishment are reached. These smallest tasks, called work packages, must be identified as manageable units that can be planned, budgeted, scheduled, and controlled. Work component descriptions often are collected in a WBS dictionary that will include work package descriptions as well as planning information, such as schedule dates, cost budgets, and staff assignments. The WBS indicates the relationship of the organizational structure to the project objectives and tasks, and so provides a firm basis for planning and controlling the project.

The WBS is first and foremost a technical data gathering structure, deployed so that the achievement in technical progress can be measured and analyzed against a formal baseline plan. The WBS aids the customer in understanding the status of the project as time elapses. The WBS aids the customer's customer in understanding the status of the project. All managers, internal and external need to use the planning and status information within the WBS structure to aide in the adjustment to the current program paths and for maximizing the attainment of short-term and long-term goals.

There are no hard-and-fast rules for preparing a WBS; good judgment is the only criterion. However, the size of these work packages is very important because they must be small enough in terms of cost and labor to permit realistic estimates to be made, and to simplify control. Many believe that the "80-hour rule" can be of tremendous help in formulating the WBS and keeping it under control. This rule states that each task should be broken down into work packages that require no more than 80 hours of work for completion. At the end of each 80-hour-or-less period, the work package is reported simply as either completed or not completed. "By means of such periodic check-ins, drifting of a project can be controlled early" (Stuckenbruck, *The Implementation of Project Management*). Other writers have mentioned the use of other "rules" for work package durations. However, PMI has used the 80-hour rule in its exam for many years. So be on the lookout for it.

BENEFITS OF USING A WBS
- Builds the project team
- Provides a framework to identify projects separately from organizations, accounting systems, and funding sources
- Clarifies responsibilities
- Focuses attention on project objectives
- Forces detailed planning and documentation
- Identifies specific work packages for estimating and assigning work

USES OF THE WBS
- Planning and budgeting
- Funding
- Estimating
- Scheduling
- Performance measurement
- Configuration management
- Integrated logistic support
- Test and performance evaluation

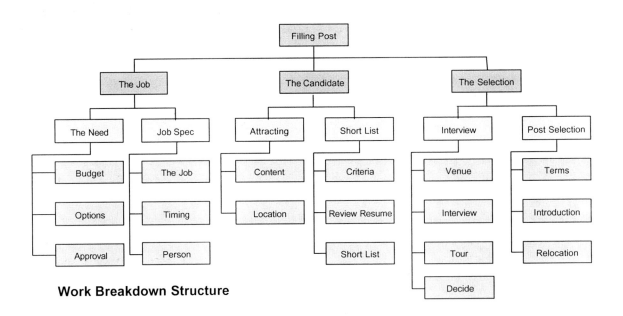

Work Breakdown Structure

DEVELOPMENT OF THE WBS

- Use Work Breakdown Structure templates
- Decomposition: This requires subdividing the major project deliverables into smaller, more manageable components until the deliverables are defined in sufficient detail to support development of project.
- Identifying the major deliverables of the project, including project management
- Deciding whether adequate cost and duration estimates can be developed in sufficient detail for each deliverable. If not, then identify constituent components of the deliverable in terms of tangible, verifiable results. When adequate detail exists, the last step is to verify the correctness of the breakdown.

To do this, you need to determine whether:

- The lower-level items are both necessary and sufficient for the broken down item
- Each item is clearly and completely defined
- Each item can be appropriately scheduled, budgeted, and assigned to an organizational unit

NOTE: You need to understand the Work Breakdown Structure for this exam. PMI currently emphasizes the product orientation to the work breakdown structure—the deliverable as orientation. Most important, you should know the Work Breakdown Structure is a decomposition of the project work that has to be done. Know how they are numbered and be able to read the numbering system and how it contributes to understanding the project. Also, be aware of the 80-hour rule. Know all of the uses, benefits, and be familiar with the fact that the Work Breakdown Structure contributes to customer communication.

OTHER STRUCTURES
Do not confuse the WBS with other types of "breakdown" structures, such as the following:

CONTRACTUAL WBS (CWBS)
This breakdown is used to define the reporting information and the timeliness of information that the supplier will give to the buyer. It is usually not as detailed as the WBS that is used to plan the work that is going to be done.

ORGANIZATIONAL BREAKDOWN STRUCTURE (OBS)
The main purpose of this structure is to show the organization of the people who will work on the project and the resources. In the OBS, the work components of the WBS are shown related to the groups of individuals and resources that will accomplish the work.

RESOURCE BREAKDOWN STRUCTURE (RBS)
This is a refinement of the OBS in that the detail of the RBS generally goes to the individual level.

BILL OF MATERIALS (BOM)
The various product components are included in the BOM in a hierarchical way. Products produced, subassemblies, and lower levels of assembly are shown as a "goes into" hierarchy.

PRODUCT BREAKDOWN STRUCTURE (PBS)
Identifies the products that are required and which must be produced by a project. This document describes the system in a hierarchical way, decomposing it through a number of levels down to the components of each product.

CONFLICT AND THE PROJECT LIFE CYCLE
The highest ranked sources of conflict evident in each phase of the life cycle are as follows:
- Concept phase - project priorities and schedules
- Development phase - project priorities, schedules and administrative procedures
- Implementation phase - schedules, technical issues, and personnel resources
- Termination phase - schedules, personality conflicts, and personnel resources

SCOPE VERIFICATION

Scope verification is the process during which project stakeholders formally sign-off on the project's scope. This process is used to gain acceptance of the current status of the project from the stakeholders. Stakeholders might review such things as completed deliverables or any current project documentation. Scope verification occurs at the end of each project life-cycle phase or when major project milestones have been completed.

It is important to understand that scope verification is a component of the project scope variable and that it is also part of the third step in the project management process–executing.

Inspection is the tool and technique used for scope verification and involves activities, such as measuring, examining, and testing that are undertaken to determine whether results conform to requirements. You should be familiar with terms that could be used for inspections, including reviews, product reviews, audits, and walkthroughs.

Formal acceptance is the output from scope verification. It is documentation that the client or the sponsor has accepted the product of the project, phase, or major deliverable. Recognize that this acceptance may be conditional, especially at the end of a phase.

NOTE: PMI wants you to know who verifies the scope and the answer is, all the critical stakeholders should verify the scope. All the key stakeholders need to have a voice in determining what is the scope, and what is going to be delivered by the project team.

SCOPE CREEP

Scope creep is a common project affliction that results from slowly adding more work over the life of the project. These changes are a problem if scope creep is so great that all of the original cost and schedule estimates become unachievable. A clear scope statement enables the project team to realize immediately that extra work is being added. Therefore, a clear scope statement is a beneficial tool to control scope creep.

When combating scope creep, it is important to realize that changes will occur during all projects. The project manager must be aware of these scope changes and compensate for them so they do not have a negative effect on the project's objectives.

DECOMPOSITION

In order to define the scope of a project, you must decompose the project deliverables. Decomposition is the process of breaking a project into manageable chunks of work, resulting in smaller deliverables that make up the final product. When decomposing a project, you begin with large chunks of work and break them down into smaller chunks so they are easy to plan, manage, and schedule. The lowest level of decomposed item is considered a work package.

PROJECT SCOPE MANAGEMENT
Risk and Complexity Trade-offs

ADVANTAGES OF DECOMPOSITION
- Estimates for cost, time, and resources are much more accurate.
- The smaller deliverables are more manageable, resulting in fewer changes being made once the project begins.
- Each project deliverable can be clearly assigned to a team member, resulting in a greater level of accountability.
- The project manager can measure team members' performance against completion of these smaller deliverables.
- Control of the project is easier, since you are dealing with smaller pieces of the overall project.

RISK AND COMPLEXITY TRADE-OFFS
Risk and uncertainty are covered extensively in a later chapter. However, there is one facet of the complexity and risk trade-off that has particular relevance to scope management. Consider the following question:

As complexity on your project increases, the level of risk or uncertainty in attempting to define the scope of the work is likely to:

A) Decrease

B) Increase

C) Remain the same

The correct answer is "b."

NOTE: For some reason people often answer these questions incorrectly on the exam. As a project becomes more complex, it becomes riskier.

SCOPE CHANGE CONTROL
Scope change control covers issues similar to integrated change control, but it focuses solely on scope changes. You should recognize that scope change requests may occur in different forms and may come from different sources:

- Oral or written
- Direct or indirect
- Externally or internally initiated
- Legally mandated or optional

The Project Management Professional (PMP®) Exam Guide   Project Scope Management **4-51**

These changes may either expand the project's scope or contract it. Changes are generally the result of:

- An external event
- An error/omission when the scope of the product or project was designed
- A value-added change
- Implementing a contingency plan or a workaround plan

A scope change is described as any modification to the agreed-upon scope as defined by the approved WBS. You should be aware that scope changes might lead to and require changes in cost, time, quality, or other project objectives. However, only project scope changes affect the performance measurement baseline. Depending on the nature of the change, the corresponding baseline document may be revised and reissued to reflect the approved change and form the new baseline for future changes. This is known as the adjusted baseline.

CHAPTER REVIEW

1. On a sensitive technology project, which of the following is an example of a value-adding change is a change that:
   A. Takes advantage of cost-reducing technology that was not available when the scope originally was defined
   B. Is caused by a new or revised government regulation
   C. Corrects omission of a required feature in the design of a system
   D. Uses a bill of materials to define the scope of the project

2. A project's payback period ends when:
   A. Unit profit is realized.
   B. Profit maximum is realized.
   C. Monthly revenue exceeds monthly costs.
   D. Cumulative revenue equals cumulative costs.

3. According to the PMBOK Guide, which of the following is an output of the scope change control process:
   A. Lessons learned
   B. Formal acceptance
   C. Work breakdown structure
   D. Scope management plan

4. The greatest degree of uncertainty is generally encountered during which phase of the project life cycle?
   A. Planning
   B. Concept
   C. Closeout
   D. Implementation

5. Management has asked you to help a key client decide which project selection method to use. The client is convinced that constrained optimization methods will work best; however, your boss believes that benefit measurement methods are more accurate. Your background is in construction management and being that this is an IT project you feel uncomfortable in advising the client on this issue. You boss has insisted you help the client so you look in the PMBOK Guide and see that all the following are examples of constrained optimization methods except:
   A. Logical framework analysis
   B. Analytic hierarchy process
   C. Multi-objective programming
   D. Economic model

6. You are the project manager for a project that was halted half way through development. You just received formal notice from the stakeholder to terminate all work. What must you do next?
    A.   Document lessons learned
    B.   Submit the work products to date to your contracting officer's technical representative
    C.   Immediately shut down the project office and reassign all personnel
    D.   Establish and document the level and extent of completion

7. The work that must be done in order to deliver a product with the specified features and functions is?
    A.   Project verification
    B.   Product scope
    C.   Project control
    D.   Project scope

8. During the concept phase of your project, management indicated that it wants the expected benefit of each new product to offset its development and production costs. This is an example of:
    A.   An assumption
    B.   A constraint
    C.   An acceptable management constraint
    D.   A management directive

9. As the senior project manager for your company you have just prepared your 200th scope statement and work breakdown structure for your company project. Management has just given you approval for the project plan. Your project is now under way and you recognize that scope change is inevitable. To avoid a similar experience, you meet with your team and decide to establish a project scope change control system, this is:
    A.   A documented process used to apply technical and administrative direction to scope changes
    B.   Mandatory for use on projects so that the scope management plan cannot be changed without prior review and sign-off
    C.   A set of procedures by which project scope may be changed, including the paperwork, tracking systems, and approval levels necessary for authorizing change
    D.   A collection of organizational procedures used to define the steps by which official project documents may be changed

10. _____ includes the process required to ensure that the project includes all the work required, and only the work required, to complete the project successfully.
    A.   Project plan update
    B.   Project scope management
    C.   Scope change control
    D.   Product description

11. The process of developing a written scope statement as the basis for future project decisions is called:
    A. Scope development
    B. Scope planning
    C. Project development
    D. Project selection

12. You are explaining to your project group about historical information and its benefits. You tell them historical information is used for which of the following?
    A. To prepare the stakeholder management plan
    B. To compare current performance with lessons learned
    C. As an input to project initiation
    D. To evaluate the skills/competencies of team members

13. As a project manager you know that project success depends on time, cost, quality, and scope control, but the primary success of any project depends on:
    A. Customer satisfaction
    B. Customer sign-off
    C. Exceeding customer needs
    D. Customer compromise in defining its needs

14. According to the PMBOK Guide, project scope management is:
    A. The features to be included in a product or service
    B. Is conducted primarily by external stakeholders
    C. Is synonymous with change control management
    D. Used to make sure that all work required, and only the work required, is included in order to complete the project successfully

15. A work breakdown structure numbering system should allow project staff to:
    A. Identify the level at which individual WBS elements are found
    B. Identify configuration management milestones
    C. Estimate the costs of the WBS elements
    D. Provide project justification

16. As senior project manager you are telling your project team that specifying the project's technical requirements is an important step because such requirements:
    A. Describe the characteristics of the deliverable
    B. Are used by the project staff to target efforts
    C. Are beneficial to both the project staff and the customers
    D. Are designed to ensure that customers know the results from a project

17. Your technical team leader has prepared a request for a value-adding change on your project that will result in expanding the project scope. To help assess the magnitude of any variations as the work to implement the change proceeds, you have mandated that earned value analysis be used. This approach represents which of the following?
    A. Performance measurement technique
    B. Configuration management process
    C. Cost accounting procedure
    D. Scope reporting mechanism

18. As lead project manager you are explaining to your team that you want to structure your project so that each project team member has a discrete work package to perform. The work package is a:
    A. Task with a unique identifier
    B. Deliverable at the lowest level of the WBS
    C. Task that can be assigned to more than one organizational unit
    D. Required level of reporting

19. Your boss has just informed you of a new government regulation and you had to change the scope of your satellite project. Several changes were made to the project's objectives and you have updated both the project's technical and planning documents. Your next step should be to:
    A. Update the work breakdown structure
    B. Notify stakeholders as appropriate
    C. Prepare a performance report
    D. Prepare a scope modification update

20. Constrained optimization methods of project selection typically include:
    A. Benefit-cost ratios for finance
    B. Scoring models for procurement
    C. Subjective computer based simulation analysis
    D. Multi-objective programming algorithms

ANSWERS

1. A
2. D
3. A
4. B
5. D
6. D
7. D
8. B
9. C
10. B
11. B
12. C
13. A
14. D
15. A
16. B
17. A
18. B
19. B
20. D

PROJECT TIME MANAGEMENT

5

The Project Time Management questions on the PMP exam focus heavily on the Program Evaluation and Review Technique (PERT), the Critical Path Method (CPM), and the Precedence Diagramming Method (PDM), and the differences between these three techniques. The exam tests your knowledge of how PERTand CPM networks are constructed, how schedules are computed, what the critical path is, and how networks are used to analyze and solve project scheduling, and resource allocation and leveling issues.

The exam may also contain some scheduling exercises. There is a focus on fast-tracking as a method to accelerate the project schedule. You must know the advantages offered by networks over bar charts and flow diagrams and understand the two ways in which networks can be represented (activity-on-arrow and activity-on-node). You should also understand the notion of float (or slack) and how it presents challenges and opportunities to project schedulers.

In the PMBOK Guide, the functions of Project Time Management are separated into five phases: activity definition, activity sequencing, duration estimating, schedule development, and schedule control. Review PMBOK Guide figure 6.1.

This knowledge area is concerned with estimating the duration of the project plan activities, devising a project schedule, and monitoring and controlling deviations from the schedule. Collectively, this knowledge area deals with completing the project in a timely manner.

In many cases, all of the activity processes described here along with schedule development are completed as one activity. Sometimes, only one person is needed to complete these five processes, and they're all worked on at the same time. Time management is an important aspect of project management as it concerns keeping the project activities on track and monitoring those activities against the project plan to assure the project is completed on time.

NOTE: As you go through this section of the exam, you do not want to spend quite as much time as you might anticipate studying the calculations associated with the whole network. Instead, what you want to look at are some unusual relationships–start-start, finish-finish, and lag and lead times, and examining the issues associated with the classical representations of schedules. That includes PERT, CPM, PDM, AOA (activity-on-arrow), and AON (activity-on-node).

ACTIVITY DEFINITION

The purpose of activity definition is to clarify the main project activities, which are outlined on the work breakdown structure. The purpose of activity sequencing is to arrange activities in a logical order for completion. As you define the project's main activities from the WBS, you should compile those activities into an activity list. The finished activity list then becomes a guide you can use during activity sequencing. Before starting activity definition, you should choose the duration estimating technique you'll use, so you know the detail level of activity definition needed for that technique.

Activity definition and sequencing are important because it ensures that no activity is omitted or left unfinished. It is also important because it includes specifying the order in which activities are to be executed. The primary input to this process is the WBS in which each work package is broken down into the activities that need to be completed to produce the deliverable.

NOTE: PMI points out that typically the WBS and the activity list are developed sequentially. The activity list should be organized as an extension to the WBS. Note that as the activity list is developed, the project team may identify missing deliverables or may decide that the deliverable descriptions need clarification. These updates are known as refinements.

PROJECT TIME MANAGEMENT

The exam tests your knowledge of the differences between PERT, CPM, and PDM (although most automated systems today treat PERT and CPM as being one and the same). The following notes highlight the individual characteristics of each of the three network systems on which you will be tested.

PERT - PROGRAM EVALUATION AND REVIEW TECHNIQUE

- Emphasis on meeting schedules with flexibility on cost
- Three time estimates per activity: pessimistic (p), most likely (m), and optimistic (o), with emphasis on most likely computed as follows: $(p + 4m + o) \div 6$
- Event oriented (slack)-activity-on-arrow

CPM - CRITICAL PATH METHOD

- Emphasis on controlling cost and keeping the schedule flexible
- One time estimate per activity
- Activity oriented (float)-activity-on-node

PDM - PRECEDENCE DIAGRAM METHOD

Represents improvement to PERT and CPM by adding lead and lag relationships to activities

- Start-to-start - relationship in a precedence diagramming method network in which one activity must start before the successor activity can start.
- Start-to-finish - relationship in a precedence diagramming method network in which one activity must start before the successor activity can finish.
- Finish-to-start - relationship in a precedence diagramming method network in which one activity must end before the successor activity can start. This is the most commonly used relationship in the precedence diagramming method.

- Finish-to-finish - relationship in a precedence diagramming method network in which one activity must end before the successor activity can end.

NOTE: You need to know what PERT, CPM and PDM are. Be prepared for questions about the Program Evaluation and Review Technique. Several questions are asked about the name itself. It will be referred to as the Program Evaluation Review Technique, the Project Evaluation Review Technique, or the Project Evaluation and Review Tactic. A variety of things will be used that fit the acronym but are not the acronym. Be sure you know exactly what PERT means.

The same thing is true with CPM. You will also want to know a little shared of history here–that this came from the 1950s and was part of the Polaris Program was U.S. Navy based and under took the task of trying to launch missiles from submarines.

Also, you will need know what PERT is and what it is based on. It is based on three estimates– the worst case, the best case, and the most likely. PMI calls those pessimistic, optimistic, and most likely. Be prepared to see it in either format: best case, worst case, and most likely; or optimistic, pessimistic, and most likely. That it is four times the mostly likely – add those numbers, and you want to divide them by six $(p + 4m + o) \div 6$. PMI uses PERT as a network diagraming approach. It uses those multidata-point durations to establish the duration of the activities.

The critical path method (also from the 1950s–remember that for the exam) works on a single data point, but it still works from the activity-on-arrow approach.

Finally, the precedence diagramming method, the one you are most familiar with, comes from Stanford University in the 1960s. Know what the different relationships mean: start-to-start, start-to-finish, finish-to-start, and finish-to-finish.

WAYS TO REPRESENT NETWORKS

ACTIVITY ON ARROW

Activity sequencing concerns the order in which activities are performed and how many sets of activities can be under way at the same time (known as parallel paths). Sequencing is important because we often need to accomplish the project as quickly as possible, yet the schedule we develop must be realistic and achievable. Activity sequencing uses the following types of dependencies:

Mandatory dependencies (hard logic): Mandatory dependencies are restrictions specific to an activity. Mandatory dependencies require that one activity be completed before another can begin. For example, when building a house, the foundation must be finished before raising the walls. Mandatory dependencies are static, which mean that they never change.

Discretionary dependencies: Discretionary dependencies, which are restrictions outlined by the project team, are based on two factors. First, if there are multiple methods of doing an activity, team members choose the best method. For example, if a team has an option to use one of two software programs, they can use the program they think best suits their needs for activity completion. Secondly, if there are many activity sequences, team members pick the one most desirable for achieving the project goals.

Discretionary dependencies can be called "soft logic." It is important to use discretionary dependencies only after careful consideration, since they can affect the activity sequence throughout the entire project.

Milestone events also need to be part of activity sequencing so that requirements for meeting the milestones are met.

You need to realize that all activities in a network diagram have at least one predecessor and one successor activity, with the exception of the start and end activities. If this convention is followed, then the sequence is relatively straightforward to identify. When you establish a project schedule, you need to compute two schedules: the early schedule, which we calculate using the forward pass; and the late schedule, which we calculate using the backward pass.

EARLY START / FORWARD PASS
The early schedule is simply the earliest time at which an activity can start and finish. These are calculated numbers that are derived from the dependencies between all the activities in the project.

LATE SCHEDULE / BACKWARD PASS
The late schedule consists of the latest times at which an activity can start and finish without delaying the completion date of the project. These are also calculated numbers that are derived from the dependencies between all of the activities in the project.

By using these two types of schedules you will determine the window of time within which each activity must be started and finished for the project to complete on schedule; and the sequence of activities that determines the project completion date. The sequence of activities that determine the project completion date is called the critical path. The critical path can be defined in several ways: 1) the longest duration path in the network diagram; 2) the sequence of activities whose early schedule and late schedule are the same; and 3) the sequence of activities with zero slack or float. All of these definitions say the same thing: what sequence of activities must be completed on schedule in order for the project to be completed on schedule.

The activities that define the critical path are called critical path activities. Any delay in a critical path activity will delay the completion of the project by the amount of delay in that activity. This is a sequence of activities that will warrant the project manager's special attention.

The earliest start (ES) time for an activity is the earliest time at which all of its predecessor activities have been completed and the subject activity can begin. The ES time of an activity with no predecessor activities is set to 1, the first day on which the project can begin production. The ES time of activities with one predecessor activity is determined from the earliest finish (EF) time of the predecessor activity. The ES time of activities having two or more predecessor activities is determined from the latest of the EF times of the predecessor activities. The EF of an activity is calculated as [(ES + duration) - one time unit]. The reason for subtracting the one time unit is to account for the fact that an activity starts at the beginning of a time unit (hour, day, and so forth) and finishes at the end of a time unit. In other words, a one-day activity, starting at the beginning of a day, begins and ends on the same day. For example, take a look at the figure below titled Forward Pass Calculations. Note that activity E has only one predecessor, activity C. The EF for activity C is the end of day 3. Because it is the only predecessor of activity E, the ES of activity E is the beginning of day 4. On the other hand, activity D has two predecessors, activity B and activity C. When there are two or more predecessors, the ES of the successor, activity D in this case, is calculated based on the maximum of the EF dates of the predecessor activities. The EF dates of the predecessors are the end of day 4 and the end of day 3. The maximum of these is 4, and therefore the ES of activity D is the morning of day 5.

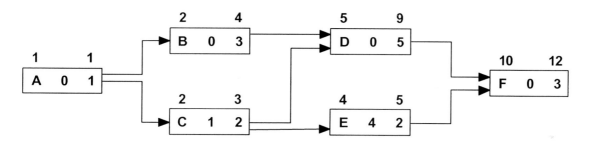

Forward Pass Calculations

The latest start (LS) and latest finish (LF) times of an activity are the latest times at which the activity can start or finish without causing a delay in the completion of the project. Knowing these times is valuable for the project manager, who must make decisions on resource scheduling that can affect completion dates. The window of time between the ES and LF of an activity is the window within which the resource for the work must be scheduled or the project completion date will be delayed.

In order to calculate these times, you have to work backward in the network diagram. First set the LF time of the last activity on the network to its calculated EF time. Its LS is calculated as ((LF - duration) + one time unit). Again, you add the one time unit to adjust for the start and finish of an activity within the same day. The LF time of all immediate predecessor activities is determined by the minimum of the LS, minus one time unit, times all of its successor activities.

Let's calculate the late schedule for activity E. (see image above) Its only successor, activity F, has an LS date of day 10. The LF date for its only predecessor, activity E, will then be the end of day 9. In other words, activity E must finish no later than the end of day 9 or it will delay the start of activity F and delay the completion date of the project. The LS date for activity E will be, using the formula, 9 - 2 + 1, or the beginning of day 8. On the other hand, consider activity C. It has two successor activities, activity D and activity E. The LS dates for them are day 5 and day 7, respectively. The minimum of those dates, day 5, is used to calculate the LF of activity C, the end of day 4. The complete calculations for the backwards pass is shown in the image below.

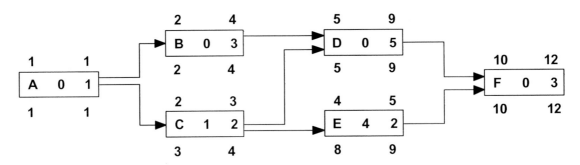

Backward Pass Calculations

THE CRITICAL PATH

The critical path is the longest path through the network. But it represents the shortest amount of time in which the project can be completed. Keep in mind that it is possible to have more than one critical path. The critical path drives the completion date of the project. Any delay in the completion of any one of the activities in the critical path sequence will delay the completion of the project. The easiest way to identify the critical path in a network diagram is to identify all possible paths through the network diagram and add up the durations of the activities.

Dummy activities are only required in activity-on-arrow networks and their purpose is to show multiple relationships or dependencies among project activities that otherwise are not in sequence. See the image on the next page for an explanation on figuring the critical path. Dummy activities consume no time or resources; they are present only to show that a dependency exists between two activities. Relationships among activities are "finish-to-start."

FIGURING THE CRITICAL PATH

Using the image on page 5-65 and assuming all duration in days

Path 1: A-D-H-J   Length = 1+4+6+3 = 14 days

Path 2: B-E-H-J   Length = 2+5+6+3 = 16 days

Path 3: E-F-J   Length = 2+4+3 = 9 days

Path 4: C-G-I-J   Length = 3+6+2+3 = 14 days

Since the critical path is the longest path through the network diagram, Path 2, B-E-H-J, is the critical path for the project.

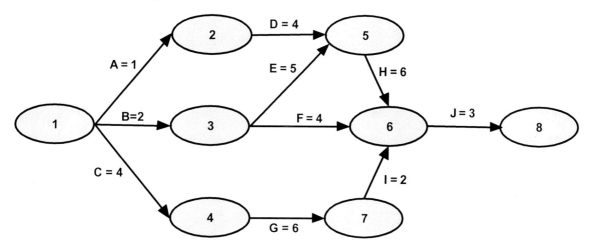

ACTIVITY-ON-NODE NETWORKS

No dummy activities are required. Activity-on-node networks incorporate lag-which is defined as waiting time between activities in a network; for example, we order something and must wait for it to arrive or we paint something and must wait for it to dry-and lead, which is defined as an acceleration of the successor task. For example, we can clean up after painting; we do not need to wait for the paint to dry.

SLACK

Slack (also called float) is the amount of time that a particular activity can be delayed without delaying the project. Activities on the critical path usually have zero slack. Slack is a calculated number and it is the difference between the late finish and the early finish (LF - EF). If the result is greater than zero, then the activity has a range of time in which it can start and finish without delaying the project completion date. There are two types of slack: free slack and total slack.

FREE SLACK

This is the span of dates in which an activity can finish without causing a delay in the early schedule of any activities that are its immediate successors. Free slack can be equal to but never greater than total slack. When you choose to delay the start of an activity, possibly for resource scheduling reasons, first consider activities that have free slack associated with them.   Notice in the figure on the next page that activity C has an early start (ES) of the beginning of day 2 and a late finish (LF) of the end of day 4. Its duration is two days and it has a 3-day window in which to be completed without affecting the early start (ES) of any of its successor activities. It therefore has free slack of only one day. If an activity's completion stays within the free slack range, it can never delay the early start date of any other activity in the project.

TOTAL SLACK

This is the range of dates in which an activity can finish without delaying the project completion date. In reviewing the diagram below look at activity E and notice that it has a free float of four days as well as a total float of four days. If Activity E were completed more than three days later than its early finish (EF) date, it would delay completion of the project. All activities on the critical path must be done on their earliest schedule or the project completion date will suffer. If an activity with total slack greater than zero were to delayed beyond its late finish (LF) date, it would become a critical path activity and cause the completion of the project to be delayed.

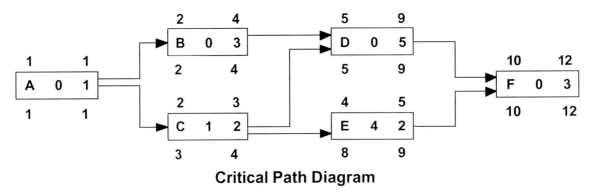

Critical Path Diagram

ACTIVITY RELATIONSHIPS

You must know the definitions of these four terms:

FINISH-TO-START

The finish to start (FS) dependency says that activity A must be completed before activity B can begin. This is the most commonly used relationship in the precedence diagramming method. For example, activity A can represent purchasing paint for a house and activity B can represent the painting of the house. To say that the dependency between A and B is finish-to-start means that once we have finished buying the paint we may start painting the house. The finish-to-start dependency is displayed with an arrow emanating from the right edge of the predecessor activity and leading to the left edge of the successor activity.

START-TO-START

The start-to-start (SS) dependency says that activity B may begin once activity A has begun. Remember that there is a no-sooner than relationship between activity A and activity B. Activity B may begin no sooner than activity A begins. Altering the example used previously we could say that as soon as we begin buying the paint for the house (activity A) we may begin painting the house (activity B). We don't need all the paint for the house in order for activity B to commence. In this case there is a start-to-start (SS) dependency between activity A and B. As seen in the illustration below, the start-to-start dependency is displayed with an arrow emanating from the left edge of the predecessor (A) and leading to the left edge of the successor (B).

FINISH-TO-FINISH

The finish-to-finish (FF) dependency states that activity B can't finish sooner than activity A. For example, painting the house (activity B) can't finish until purchasing all the paint for the house (activity A) is completed. In this case, activity A and B have a finish-to-finish dependency. The finish-to-finish dependency is displayed with an arrow emanating from the right edge of activity A to the right edge of activity B.

START-TO-FINISH

The start-to-finish (SF) dependency is a little more complex than the finish-to-start and the start-to-start dependencies. Here activity B can not be finished sooner than activity A has started. For example, suppose your business organization has adopted a new computer network. You wouldn't want to eliminate the old system until the new system is operable. When the new network starts to work (activity A) the old system can be discontinued (activity B). The start-to-finish dependency is displayed with an arrow emanating from the left edge of activity A to the right edge of activity B as seen in the illustration on the next page.

TASK DEPENDENCIES

The nature of the relationship between two linked tasks. You link tasks by defining a dependency between their finish and start dates, For example, the "contact caterers" task must finish before the start of the "determine menus" tasks. There are four kinds of task dependencies.

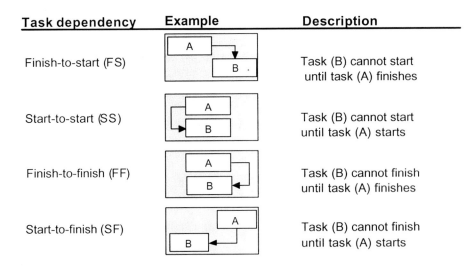

Task dependency	Example	Description
Finish-to-start (FS)		Task (B) cannot start until task (A) finishes
Start-to-start (SS)		Task (B) cannot start until task (A) starts
Finish-to-finish (FF)		Task (B) cannot finish until task (A) finishes
Start-to-finish (SF)		Task (B) cannot finish until task (A) starts

NOTE: This material is extremely important and most likely you will see at least six or seven questions relating to this information on the exam.

We will start with activity-on-arrow, which works with activity sequencing. It is always a finish-to-start relationship. Activity A must finish before Activity B can start. In activity-on-arrow diagrams, there are sometimes "dummy" activities.

The critical path is an important element here, and you will have a couple of questions on it. The critical path is the shortest time in which the project can possibly be accomplished. It is also referred to as the longest path through a network. It is the shortest period in which the project can be completed. Thus, it is the longest path through the network.

Activity-on-node networks also allow you the latitude of putting in lag. Know that slack is a synonym for float. However, float and slack are not the same thing as lag. Lag is something we assign when we want a delay. Slack or float describes what the function of a network is.

Memorize the relationships in the task dependency diagram.

CONDITIONAL DIAGRAMMING METHODS

Because PDM and ADM do not allow loops (such as tests that must be repeated more than once) or conditional branching (such as a design update that is only needed if the inspection detects errors), in these situations, conditional diagramming methods such as the Graphical Evaluation and Review Technique (GERT) and systems dynamics models must be used. GERT allows for probabilistic treatment of both network logic and activity duration estimates. Here, some activities may not be performed at all, some may only be partially performed, and others may be performed more than once. GERT combines signal flow graph theory, probabilistic networks, PERT/CPM, and decision trees into a single framework. Its components consist of logical nodes and directed arcs or branches. GERT and its various enhancements are computer simulations and as such they are difficult to use as a control tool. For purposes of the exam, you need to know only how GERT differs from PDM and ADM. No exercise or example is provided from which you have to compute dates and the like.

ACTIVITY DURATION ESTIMATING

When developing a duration estimate for an activity, we are primarily concerned with identifying how many "work periods" the activity will take and its elapsed time. The estimate is based on the following:

- Number of resources assigned
- capability of those resources to do the job
- Prior results

The person or group that is most familiar with the work should develop, or at least approve, the estimate.

During the estimating process, the project team also must consider information on identified risks. This involves the extent to which the effect of risks is included in the baseline duration estimate for each activity, including risks with high probabilities for impact.

You should be familiar with the tools and techniques used to estimate activity durations:

- Expert judgment
- Analogous or top-down estimating
- Quantitatively based durations: Quantities to be performed for each work category multiplied by the productivity unit rate
- Reserve time (contingency). Note that PMI states that project teams may choose to incorporate an additional time frame, reserve contingency, or buffer that can be added to the activity duration or elsewhere in the schedule as recognition of the schedule risk.Later, when more information about the project is available, this reverse time can be reduced or eliminated.
- Parametric estimate – A mathematical model that uses parameters, or project characteristics, to forecast project costs.

Duration estimates using PERT are more pessimistic (PMI uses the word "realistic") than the single time estimate used in original CPM calculations. This is because the PERT approach was built on the beta distribution and was specifically designed to overcome the optimism often found in schedule estimates.

PMI recommends that duration estimates always include some indication of the range of possible results (for example, 2 weeks plus or minue 2 days or 85 percent probability that the activity will take less than 3 weeks). This is called range estimating.

SCHEDULE DEVELOPMENT

Schedule development is the process by which a project manager incorporates the project's main activities from a network diagram into a schedule. The purpose of project scheduling is to ensure that effective time management occurs during the project and that a project is completed within a reasonable amount of time. During schedule development, the project manager assigns a start and end date to each activity. It is critical to consider such things as activity relationships, activity duration, and resource availability when developing a project schedule.

Critical inputs are the project network diagram and the activity duration estimates. Project calendars (which affect all resources) and resource calendars (which affect only a specific resource or category of resources) must be considered when developing the schedule. Be familiar also with two categories of time constraints: imposed dates and key events or major milestones.

IMPOSED DATES

A project completion date might be imposed by an outside entity. For example, if a judge orders a landlord to make repairs at an apartment complex, the judge can dictate a date by which time all repairs must be made. If the repairs are not made by that date, the landlord might have to pay fines.

KEY EVENTS / MILESTONES

The second constraint to consider during development is the time frame expectations of project stakeholders. Since stakeholders expect to see progress, it is valuable to include milestones on project network diagrams and schedules. The milestones enable stakeholders to verify that progress has been made.

Other key inputs are the risk management plan and activity attributes, including responsibility and geographic area.

CRASHING AND FAST-TRACKING

Both crashing and fast-tracking are ways to speed things up when schedule pressures exist or when the project is falling behind schedule. The focus is always on critical path activities because it is those activities that determine the length of the project.

CRASHING

Crashing involves adding more resources to activities on the critical path in order to accomplish the work faster.

The following is the recommended approach to crashing a network:

- Compute the critical path.
- Establish an objective total duration.
- Identify the crash time and crash cost for each activity on the critical path.
- Prioritize the activities on the critical path that can be shortened at minimum cost.
- Shorten the highest priority activity by one time period and compare total duration with objective.
- Verify the critical path.
- Continue activity reduction until crash time is reached.
- Select next priority activity and continue reduction.

NOTE: Remember that crashing the network almost always increases project costs!

FAST-TRACKING

Fast-tracking involves analyzing the critical path to see which activities could be done in parallel (as opposed to sequential execution). It also involves more aggressive use of such PDM activity relationships as start-to-start so that subsequent activities can begin before the prior activity has been completed. This overlapping also reduces the project schedule. It is similar to crashing in that it usually requires more resources to make it happen. Fast-tracking often results in rework.

NOTE. This approach usually increases risk, because of the greater coordination required to monitor and control multiple, concurrent activities.

When it comes to these two issues, you need to be able to differentiate between the two besides knowing the process. The difference between crashing and fast-tracking is that crashing compresses the time on given activities on the critical path. Fast-tracking looks at doing activities in parallel. Also, you need to know the difference between fast-tracking and concurrent engineering. Fast-tracking is when you do tasks in parallel. When you do concurrent engineering, you are doing whole phases and tasks in parallel.

RESOURCE LEVELING

The goal of resource leveling is to optimize the use of people and equipment assigned to the project. It begins with the assumption that, when possible, it is more productive to have consistent, continuous use of the fewest resources possible. In other words, it seeks to avoid repeatedly adding and removing resources throughout the project. Resource leveling is the last step in creating a realistic schedule. It confronts the reality of limited people and equipment, and adjusts the schedule to compensate.

Let us consider a few of the problems faced by project managers in the process of leveling resources. As you are aware, every project faces the reality of limited people and equipment. The idea is to avoid both over and under allocation.

Project managers need to remember that whether its people or equipment, there are rarely a bunch of spares sitting around waiting to be used. Those over-allocation problems can become especially acute if project managers imagine that they have a large supply of rare resources, such as unlimited time of the only subject matter expert.

The other side of the problem is under allocation. If the project team is not busy on your project, it will likely be reassigned to other projects and be unavailable when the next peak comes.

A further problem arises if people working on this project are also working on several others at the same time. If every project in the firm has wild swings in its resources, it is almost impossible to move people smoothly between projects. Instead, people are yanked off one project to help another catch up, only to be thrown at another that is even further behind.

Project managers must do their best to avoid resource peaks and valleys, and try to use a consistent set of people on the project at a consistent rate. This is not only more realistic, it is more efficient, because every upswing in resources has a cost, whether it comes from procuring additional equipment or transporting new team members to a site. The learning cost can be the steepest. On knowledge projects, the learning curve can be so long that adding additional developers for only a few weeks can actually result in negative productivity.

Resource leveling involves scheduling the project in a way that uses resources most effectively. By using positive float available on non-critical paths through the project, the project planner can arrange a schedule of work that accomplishes the same result in the same time while smoothing or leveling the peaks and valleys in the resources to be consumed. Float, then, is considered a "project resource." Resource leveling generally results in a schedule that is longer in duration than the preliminary schedule. The reason for this stems from the fact that when most people develop a preliminary schedule, they assume that each resource required to complete any activity is available at the early start date, and that the number of resources is also required. Thus, when a resource leveling exercise is undertaken, the actual number of resources, and their availability, is factored into the schedule, which generally results in a schedule that is longer in duration than the preliminary one. Two types of constrained scheduling techniques are:

RESOURCE-CONSTRAINED SCHEDULE

The network schedule is allowed to change, based on the availability of identified resources.

TIME-CONSTRAINED SCHEDULE

The network schedule is fixed. The absence of required resources per activity is indicated by negative float.

Additionally, you should be familiar with the following approaches:

RESOURCE-BASED METHOD

One in which resources are reallocated from non-critical to critical activities in order to bring the schedule back, or as close as possible, to its original intended overall duration.

REVERSE RESOURCE ALLOCATION

Used on projects that have a finite and critical project resource that must be scheduled in reverse from the project's end date.

CRITICAL CHAIN

A technique popularized by Eli Goldratt that is used to modify the project schedule to account for limited resources and to incorporate buffers to reduce schedule risk. Because random events occur that cause some project activities to be late, activity buffers are introduced. They do not solve the problem, so a project buffer is required. Then another problem occurs: paths that feed into the critical path may be late; and this in turn may cause the critical path to be delayed. Feeding buffers now must be used. However, still there may be a problem because a scarce resource may be used by the critical path and by feeding paths. The approach to follow, therefore, is to set up a schedule to allocate scarce resources by an equivalent to the minimum slack heuristic, except that the slack includes all the relevant buffers. The critical chain is the sequence in which the scarce resource activities are processed.

Be familiar with the intended use of each of the following four resource planning tools:

RESPONSIBILITY ASSIGNMENT MATRIX

Used to identify who does what. A matrix that lists what work must be done on one side and who is responsible for doing it on the other side.

RESOURCE SPREADSHEET

Quantifies how much effort is needed from each resource on the project during each time period.

RESOURCE GANTT CHART

Borrows the Gantt chart concept to identify the precise periods of time when a particular resource is working on a particular task.

RESOURCE HISTOGRAM

A vertical bar chart that shows the total number of resources needed during each time period of the project.

When compared to the number of resources that will actually be available, this planning tool is designed to identify any time periods for which insufficient resources are available. The idea is to work out these problems ahead of time so they do not cause problems or surprise the project manager during the course of the project.

WBS activities ⟶

OBS units	1.1.1	1.1.2	1.1.3	1.1.4	1.1.5	1.1.6	1.1.7	1.1.8
System Engineering	R	RP					R	
Software Development			RP					
Hardware Development				RP				
Test Engineering	P							
Quality Assurance					RP			
Config. Management						RP		
Integrated Support							P	
Training								RP

R = Responsible organizational unit
P = Performing organizational unit

NOTE: When it comes to resource leveling, remember that it is the reduction of the over-commitment of resources. That is what you are trying to do. You are trying to use resources most effectively. Resource smoothing involves roughly the same thing. Leveling involves, easing up on the commitment of resources, and smoothing involves trying to create some equilibrium among resources.

In a resource-constrained schedule, leveling means that the network schedule is generally going to be extended. If you are cutting back on your resources' hours, generally it is going to take longer to complete the project. By contrast, in a time-constrained schedule, often leveling will result in a negative float. It will result in us moving out past the schedule due date, which means that we have a negative float. We have to make some kind of network correction to go back and resolve the conflict that is involved.

MONTE CARLO ANALYSIS

Monte Carlo Analysis uses the power of a computer to simulate the project outcomes many times. It yields a range of possible outcomes (cost and schedule are usually of particular interest) and provides the probability for each outcome. This process gives a project manager much better information for planning a project.

HEURISTIC SCHEDULING (RULE OF THUMB)

Heuristics are rules of thumb or guidelines that have been learned through experience and trial and error. An example of a heuristic is the PERT process, which has modified some statistical approaches to create a simpler but useful scheduling process; for example, the PERT formula for standard deviation is a heuristic (simple to use but yields good results).

Heuristics, as defined by Webster's Dictionary, is learning by discovery. It is simple trial and error. We use heuristics in scheduling when we are trying to work from past experience. PERT is a good example of a heuristic, because it looks at the worst case, the best case, and the most likely, and works with those parameters to establish some standard deviation.

ADVANTAGES OF SCHEDULING TOOLS

There are particular advantages to each tool. If you are working with networks, they are going to give you a sense of the relationships between activities–which ones comes first, how they interact, and how they are related. Networks also give you the critical path.

BAR CHART (GANTT CHART)

- Weak planning tool but effective progress reporting tool
- Easy to read
- No logical relationships between or among activities

MILESTONE CHART

- Shows significant events on the project
- Identifies only scheduled start or completion of major deliverables
- Good for communicating status with customers and upper management
- Milestones have zero duration

NETWORKS (PERT, CPM, PDM)

- Show how project activities and events are related
- Identify critical path, project duration, and activity sequences

PMI tends to think of the Gantt chart as this terrible useful tool, but for the exam you need to be aware that the bar chart or Gantt chart is considered an extremely weak planning tool. It is not a good planning tool, although you may use it every day. It is a fine progress-reporting tool. It works very well for reporting progress but not very well in terms of planning.

Milestone charts are good for the high-level perspective. They show significant events, and remember that a milestone is an activity of zero duration. It has no duration. They may try and trick you into believing that there is some reason you might want a milestone to have some duration.

The best way to know if it is a milestone is, could it be expressed in the past tense in one way or another? If it can't—if it involves some activity or some time passing—it is not a true milestone.

SCHEDULE MANAGEMENT PLAN

Project managers cannot arbitrarily make changes to a schedule. A schedule management plan provides guidelines for project managers to follow when making changes to a project schedule. Schedule management plans are not necessarily formal or highly detailed, but should give enough detail to provide guidance when scheduling changes arise.

SCHEDULE CONTROL

From a time management point of view, time control or project control is about the schedule baseline and any changes that might occur. The schedule baseline is the original, approved project schedule and becomes the standard used to measure schedule performance. The baseline should never be changed without proper review and approval.

Change requests may occur in numerous ways but any approved change should be documented in writing. Changes may either extend or accelerate the schedule. Changes almost always increase the project cost!

NOTE: Control is a big issue with PMI, and when it comes to project schedule control, it is the same issue as with project cost control and project scope control. Control is governed by the baseline. You use a schedule baseline, you establish that baseline, and that is the original approved project schedule. Any variance to the schedule is going to be reflected against that schedule. Any change requests are going to be evaluated against that original baseline.

VARIANCE ANALYSIS

Variance analysis is a key tool and technique for schedule control. The general formula for any kind of variance is Plan-Actual. Therefore, if a task was planned to take four days and it actually takes five days, the schedule variance (SV) would be equal to -1 day. If the SV is a positive number, then more work was completed than originally planned up to that point. If the SV is a negative number, then less work was completed than originally planned up to that point. The earned value formula for schedule variance follows:

- $SV = EV - PV$ or
- $SV = BCWP - BCWS$
- Where EV is the earned value or the budgeted cost of work performed
- And PV is the planned value or budgeted cost of work scheduled

NOTE: This schedule variance formula is thoroughly tested in the Project Time Management section of the exam. See Project Cost Management, for a detailed review of the Earned Value Technique.

Comparing target dates with the actual and forecast start and finish dates provides useful information for the detection of deviations and for the implementation of corrective solutions in case of delays. Pay attention to the float variance and to critical and subcritical activities (for example, analyzing the ten subcritical paths in order of ascending float).

SCHEDULE UPDATES

Sometimes schedules need to be changed or updated to reflect such things as changes in activity sequence or resource redistribution. It is important to keep a project's schedule up-to-date so team members can verify their activity completion times and resource constraints.

A revision is a type of schedule update. Revisions are alterations of a project's original start and completion dates. Most often, revisions are made based on changes to the project's scope. Rebaselining may be required if schedule delays are severe. Use rebaselining only as a last resort for schedule control; new target schedules should be the normal mode of schedule revision.

CORRECTIVE ACTION

Corrective action may be needed as a result of schedule control. This often involves expediting special actions to ensure completion of an activity on time or with the least possible delay. Root cause analysis may be needed to identify the causes of the variation.

CHAPTER REVIEW

1. The inputs to schedule control include all of the following except:
    A. Performance reports
    B. Project schedule
    C. Corrective action
    D. Schedule management plan

2. When developing a project schedule, you want to define a distribution of probable results for each activity and use it to calculate a distribution of probable results for the total project, the easiest way to do this is:
    A. Monte Carlo analysis
    B. PERT
    C. Pareto analysis
    D. GERT

3. What is the network analysis technique called that shows conditional and probabilistic treatment of logical relationships?
    A. ADM
    B. CPM
    C. GERT
    D. PERT

4. Which tools or techniques are not used in activity sequencing:
    A. Precedence diagramming method (PDM)
    B. Arrow diagramming method (ADM)
    C. Expert judgment
    D. Network templates

5. Which process is not included in project time management:
    A. Activity sequencing
    B. Work breakdown structure development
    C. Schedule development
    D. Activity definition

6. Which of the following is not true concerning the tools and techniques of activity sequencing:
    A. GERT allows for loops
    B. GERT uses analogous methods
    C. GERT allows for conditional branches
    D. GERT is a conditional diagramming method

7. A resource pool description provides which of the following:
   A. The unit cost for each resource
   B. What resources will be available, at what times, and in what numbers
   C. Performance of the pool resources
   D. Resource requirements for each element of the WBS

8. When using a network diagram, a loop means which of the following:
   A. Allows several activities to be repeated in sequential order
   B. Allows for elimination of unproductive tasks not to be repeated
   C. A network path that passes the same node twice
   D. All paths meet at the last activity in the diagram

9. Which tools or techniques are not used in activity sequencing:
   A. Arrow diagramming method ADM
   B. Precedence diagramming method PDM
   C. Network templates
   D. Expert judgment

10. A method of shortening the duration of the project by doing activities in parallel is:
    A. Creating milestones
    B. Fast tracking
    C. Leveling
    D. Lead

11. An activity has an optimistic duration estimate of two days, a mostly likely estimate of five days, and a pessimistic estimate of eight days. What is the weighted average duration?
    A. 5
    B. 4
    C. 7
    D. 6

12. You have been working on a complex project for your company. Your boss has asked you what the duration is going to be to complete one certain task. You respond that the most optimistic time for the task to be completed is five days. You made some additional notes stating that you feel the longest the task would take is fifteen days, that the most likely period is ten days, and the average time for completing the task based on previous work is usually eight days. If you use PERT, what is the expected duration of the task?
    A. 9 days
    B. 8 days
    C. 11 days
    D. 10 days

13. The project office just issued you a project review summary. Your eyes immediately notice "recommendations" in the executive summary. You have been criticized for failing to provide sufficient supporting detail about the project. Although the report does not provide examples, you remember reading about supporting detail in the PMBOK Guide. It includes all the following except:
   - A. Cash-flow projections
   - B. Order and delivery schedules
   - C. Management position papers
   - D. Best-and worst-case alternative schedules

14. According to the WBS, a task was scheduled to be completed in three weeks using two people, but was actually completed in four weeks using one person. What is the coat variance of this task?
   - A. + 50 %
   - B. - 50%
   - C. + 100%
   - D. - 100%

15. The required inputs for schedule control include all except:
   - A. Change requests
   - B. Performance reports
   - C. Project network diagram
   - D. A schedule management plan

16. Which of the following formulas will provide the best result for computing activity duration?
   - A. AD = Work quantity ÷ Number of resources
   - B. AD= Production rate * Work quantity ÷ Number of resources
   - C. AD = Production rate ÷ Work quantity
   - D. AD = Work quantity ÷ Production rate

17. Project managers need to pay attention to critical and subcritical activities when evaluating project time performance. One way to do this is to analyze ten subcritical paths in order of ascending float. This approach is part of:
   - A. Variance analysis
   - B. Simulation
   - C. Corrected value management
   - D. Resource analysis

18. A precedence diagram and an arrow diagram are both examples of networks. What is the primary difference between them?
   - A. Arrow diagram incorporates PERT in the activity duration
   - B. Precedence diagram represents activities as nodes
   - C. Arrow diagram does not indicate critical path
   - D. Precedence diagram uses float as part of the activity duration

19. Adjusting resources applied to maintain constant resource loading is called?
    A. Leveling
    B. Crashing
    C. Restructuring
    D. Floating

20. Decomposition is a technique that is used in both scope and activity definition. Which statement describes the role decomposition plays in activity definition as compared to scope definition?
    A. Final output is described in terms of work packages
    B. Decomposition is used the same way in both activities
    C. Final output is described as deliverables items
    D. Final output is described as activities or action steps

ANSWERS

1. C
2. A
3. C
4. C
5. B
6. B
7. B
8. C
9. D
10. B
11. A
12. D
13. C
14. A
15. C
16. D
17. A
18. B
19. A
20. D

PROJECT COST MANAGEMENT

· ·

6

You do not have to be an accountant to successfully answer the project Cost Management question on the PMP exam. PMI addresses cost management from a project manager's perspective, which is extremely general.

You will probable be questions relating to contract cost management. Because cost considerations are heavily affected by contract type and Project Procurement Management, this is one of the nine areas on which you will be heavily tested. PMI also discusses performance reporting, including earned value analysis, in Project Communications Management. So, time spent studying that portion of Project Communications Management also will help prepare you for the Project Cost Management questions.

As its name implies Project Cost Management focuses on costs and budgets. The processes that make up this knowledge area are: Resource Planning, Cost Estimating, Cost Budgeting, and Cost Control.

The activities in the Project Cost Management area establish estimates for costs and resources and keep watch over those costs to ensure that the project stays within the approved budget. Depending on the complexity of the project these processes might need to involve more than one person. For example, the finance person might not have expertise in resource planning, so the project manager will need to bring in a staff member with those skills to complete the resource planning process.

LIFE CYCLE COST (LCC)

The life cycle cost of an item or a system is the total cost of acquiring (designing, producing, installing, testing, and so on), operating, and maintaining that item or system over its entire life, and disposing of the product at the end of its useful life. Some people refer to this idea as the total cost of ownership. Although some of the life cycle costs are normally incurred after the project is complete, PMI has recently advocated that project teams consider taking any actions that may be necessary to reduce this overall cost of ownership. PMI also states that life cycle costing and value engineering techniques are used to reduce cost and time, improve quality and performance, and optimize the decision—making process.

PMI states that predicting and analyzing the prospective financial performance of the project's product often is done outside of the project. In some applications, though, this is part of project cost management. If these predictions and analyses are included, project cost management then includes additional processes and numerous general management techniques including return on investment, discounted cash flow analysis, and payback analysis.

For example, if the project product is a new kind of car, it is possible that the cost of the product life cycle would increase if a decision were made to decrease the number of tests run on the engine of the car. Since fewer tests would be run, customers would probably have to make engine repairs more frequently, resulting in higher costs to operate the product.

TYPES OF RESOURCES

Several types of resources are used to complete projects:

- People are the most common resources needed to complete a project. Team members are needed for nearly every aspect of most projects.
- Facilities are needed to house the work for many projects. Offices, conference rooms, presentation rooms, and workrooms are a few examples of facilities used for projects. Frequently, these facilities can drive the project schedule according to their availability.
- Equipment is frequently needed to complete the project work. Again, equipment can drive the project schedule according to availability.
- Expenses, such as travel, room and board, and supplies are important resources to consider.
- Materials are necessary resources when the project deliverable is a physical product.

RESOURCE PLANNING

How many and what resources are required? What skill level is required of those resources? What affect will the resource have on costs?

Resource Planning establishes resource requirements by analyzing the activities in the WBS. To determine the resources needed for a project, you begin by researching past projects that required similar activities, documenting the skill sets that were utilized, and verifying those skill sets with people who actually worked on the project.

This establishes a basis for resource usage throughout the project.

- The Work Breakdown Structure is the primary input to resource planning.
- Knowledge of what resources are potentially available is necessary. The amount of detail and level of specificity of the resource pool description will vary.
- Resource requirements are the outputs of this process and should be stated in terms of the types of resource and quantities for each element in the lowest level of the Work Breakdown Structure.

FUNDAMENTALS OF COST ESTIMATING

Cost estimating is a project variable that is primarily concerned with the cost of the resources needed for a project and focuses on making sure that a project is completed within an identified budget. Costs must be estimated for all resources that are charged to the project.

Recognize that cost estimating is not pricing. Cost estimating involves developing an assessment of the likely quantitative result, whereas pricing involves a business decision—how much the performing organization will charge for the product or service. Pricing uses the cost estimate as one of many considerations.

WORK BREAKDOWN STRUCTURE

The PMBOK Guide indicates that the WBS identifies project activities that will need resources and will, therefore, require expenditures. The WBS also identifies all the work that must be scheduled and that will require expenditures. You will recall that the lowest level of project activity is known as the work package. A cost account or a control account is one level above the work package and is used for monitoring and controlling purposes. PMI explains that a control account plan (CAP) is a management control point at which the integration of scope, budget, and schedule takes place, and at which performance is measured. CAPs are placed at selected points on the WBS. The chart of accounts is provide to describe the coding structure, used by the organization, to report financial information to its general ledger. Project cost estimates must be assigned to the correct accounting category. The project team should consider the extent to which the effect of risk is included in the cost estimates for each activity.

RESOURCE RATES

Effective cost estimations require knowledge of the resources that are needed, as well as the rate charged for each resource. For example, if it takes twelve team members ten days to complete a work package, their wage rate must be known up front in order to estimate the cost of that work package. Or, if the project goal is to produce a new PMP software application and put 15,000 CD-ROM copies on the market, the cost per CD-ROM must be known ahead of time in order to estimate the cost of reaching that goal.

CHART OF ACCOUNTS

Once all the cost approximations are complete for a project, these costs must be arranged correctly according to the organization's accounting department. A chart of accounts is a list of codes that are assigned to the various costs of a project. Each individual cost account generally represents a specific work package in the WBS, making it easy to monitor performance on a daily, weekly or monthly basis.

COST ESTIMATING TECHNIQUES

ANALOGOUS ESTIMATING / OR TOP-DOWN ESTIMATING

Analogous estimating is based on historical data and comparisons with similar projects within the group or company. For example, if the company had a project two years ago that was similar to the current project, then the actual cost of the previous estimate, adjusted for inflation, might be used.

Parametric models are often used to extrapolate data from one project to fit another. It is most appropriate to use analogous estimating for top level planning and decision making. This type of estimate is accurate to within -10 percent and +25 percent. It should be noted that analogous estimating is good enough for planning, but not good enough for a final estimate.

PARAMETRIC MODELING

This type of estimating relies on knowledge of mathematical relationships between two or more characteristics of a project. For example, accurate cost estimates can be obtained for house construction through historical knowledge of the statistical relationship of dollars per square foot/meter. Similarly, one might collect information on dollars per line of code for software development projects or on dollars per lane mile/kilometer in highway construction.

- A commonly used statistical technique for modeling such relationships is known as regression analysis. The relationship is graphically represented on a scatter diagram. The regression line on the diagram estimates the average value for the dependent variable corresponding to each value of the independent variable.
- A real-world example of a parametric model that sometimes relies on regression analysis is called the learning curve. The learning curve mathematically models the intuitive notion that the more times we do something, the faster we will be able to perform the task. Specifically, learning curve theory says that each time we double the number of times we have done something; the time it takes to perform the task will decrease in a regular pattern. The regression modeling process is able to determine the rate at which the decrease occurs.

BOTTOM-UP ESTIMATING

The bottom-up estimating method is the most accurate of the three methods. It is based on the work package level (lowest level) of the work breakdown structure and requires costing each package or task. Estimates are determined by the person who performs the task and the project manager should contact the person who will actually complete the task and ask him how long it will take to do the task and what the cost will be.

ACCURACY OF ESTIMATES

PMI offers the following guidelines for the accuracy of cost estimates:

- Order-of-magnitude estimates are approximations without detailed data, often done early in a project when a "ballpark guesstimate" is needed. Such estimates have an accuracy range of -25 percent to +75 percent.
- Budget estimates are based on slightly better data and are often used to establish initial funding and gain project approval. The range of accuracy is -10 percent to +25 percent.
- Definitive estimates are prepared from well-defined, detailed data. A bottom-up estimate would be an example of a definitive estimate, which is the most accurate (with a range of -5 percent to +10 percent).

NOTE: Memorize these three types of estimating before taking the exam.

When it comes to cost estimating, you can anticipate a number of questions specifically focusing on the idea that the WBS is still the best way to go, and the best tool you have when it comes to cost estimating. Why? Because the WBS supports bottom-up estimate. The WBS is critical to cost estimating because we estimate the activities, how much they are going to cost at the work package level, and then we roll them up to the cost accounts.. PMI also feels that this is the best method.

Analogous estimates are equally important. You will need to know what they are for the exam and that they are referred to as a type of top-down estimate. For the exam, think of analogous estimates as being top-down estimates.

Parametric estimating uses a variety of functions and tools that, in the end, come up with an estimate. Specifically, it is a formula used to express a mathematical relationship between the project and the dollars that are going to be invested in that project.

Accuracy of estimates actually shows up on the exam. You can anticipate a number of questions associated with the accuracy levels of the different types of estimates. Specifically, what you can expect is order of magnitude estimates to be described as +75/-25 percent.

Budget estimates have a greater accuracy rate: +25/-10 percent. Budget estimates, remember, are also known as top-down estimates.

Definitive estimates are bottom-up estimates. They are the WBS estimates. Definitive estimates have an accuracy range of +10/-5 percent.

TRIANGULAR DISTRIBUTION

Triangular distribution is used only when we know the minimum, maximum and most likely values. It leads to a less conservative estimate of uncertainty. The triangular distribution is useful for stochastic modeling rather than statistical analysis because of its artificial nature.

Distribution Formula: Probability (cost < most likely) = (most likely - min) ÷ (max - min)

BASICS OF COST MANAGEMENT TERMINOLOGY

The law of diminishing returns identifies a situation in which you are putting more and more of something (dollars, people, and so on) into your project, and then getting proportionately less and less out of it.

Variable versus fixed costs: Variable costs rise directly with the size of the project (for example, the costs associated with skilled labor or materials consumed directly by the project). Fixed costs do not change because you decide to produce fifty more units. Fixed costs are non-recurring expenses associated with putting a production line in place.

Direct versus indirect costs: Direct costs are incurred directly by a specific project and usually include such items as salaries of project staff (project manager and full-time functional experts), materials used directly on the project, subcontractor expenses, and so on. Indirect costs are part of the overall organization's cost of doing business and are shared (allocated to) among all the projects that are under way. These costs include such things as security guards, electricity, fringe benefits, insurance, tax, and in general, anything that would be considered part of overhead.

Contingency/management reserve: The word reserve is often used with a modifier (for example, contingency reserve or management reserve) in order to provide further detail on what types of risk are being mitigated. The PMBOK Guide defines contingency reserve as the amount of money or time needed above the estimate that reduces the risk of overruns of project objectives to a level acceptable to the organization. For example, rework is certain; the amount of rework is not. Contingency reserves may involve cost, schedule, or both. Contingency reserves are intended to reduce the impact of missing cost or schedule objectives. They are normally included in the project's cost and schedule baselines. Management reserves are separately planned quantities used to allow for future situations that are impossible to predict (sometimes called "unknown unknowns"). Management reserves may involve costs or schedules. They are intended to reduce the risks of missing costs or schedule objectives. The use of a management reserve requires a change to the project's cost baseline. The purpose of a reserve is to reduce the chances of a cost-to-time overrun when risks turn into problems. Remember, in some application areas the definitions of management reserves and contingency reserves are exactly the opposite of those presented above. The important point for test-taking purposes is that you know what a reserve is and why one exists.

NOTE: The risk management plan often includes cost contingency, which can be determined on the basis of the expected accuracy of the estimate so the risk management plan serves as an input to cost budgeting.

DEPRECIATION OF CAPITAL

When money is spent to purchase capital equipment, there are several ways to write off these expenses from taxable income.

The straight-line method takes an equal credit during each year of the useful life of the equipment.

There are two methods of accelerated depreciation that are used for writing off the expense even faster than the straight-line approach: double declining balance and sum-of-the-year's digits. You do not need to know the formulas, just their names.

VALUE ANALYSIS

Value analysis is a cost reduction tool that involves careful analysis of a design or item to identify all the functions as well as the cost of each function. The approach then considers whether the function is really necessary and whether it can be provided at a lower cost without degrading performance or quality. It is also a technique used in product analysis.

COST RISK AND CONTRACT TYPE

This subject is covered more thoroughly in the section titled Project Risk Management. However, you might see several questions on the exam about which party to a contract bears the cost risk. The idea is simple and you can answer any question on this subject if you know the following:

- With a **fixed-price contract,** the seller is legally obligated to deliver the product or service described in the contract. This requirement holds true even if the contractor spends more money than expected in fulfilling the contract. Therefore, with a fixed-price contract, the seller bears the cost risk.
- Conversely, with a **cost-reimbursement contract**, the cost risk is borne by the customer. This is true because in such a contract the buyer agrees to cover the contractor's costs plus an agreed-upon amount of profit. Also, in such contractual arrangements, the contractor is legally required to provide only its "best effort" in fulfilling the contract deliverables.

NOTE: For this section know that the seller has the biggest risk in a fixed-price contract. Likewise, in a cost-reimbursement or cost-plus contract, the big risk is going to be borne by the customer.

COST MANAGEMENT PLAN

A cost management plan is developed to provide guidelines for the project manager to follow when dealing with cost variances. The amount of detail included in a cost management plan is dependent on the needs of the project stakeholder. The plan should outline steps that need to be taken if the actual project costs are higher or lower than the approved project budget.

To make a cost management plan useful, the accumulated costs of the project must always be available by looking at the cost baseline, which is displayed as an S-curve. The project stakeholders can then compare the approved budget to the cost baseline to determine if the project costs are on target.

COST BUDGETING

Cost budgeting is the process of allocating cost to the individual work items in the project. Project performance will be determined based on the budget allocated to the various parts of the project. The result of the cost budgeting process is the cost baseline of the project. The cost baseline for the project is the expected actual cost of the project.

The cost baseline is the output of cost budgeting. It is a time-phased budget that is used to measure and monitor cost performance. Be aware that many projects may have multiple cost baselines that are used to measure different aspects of cost performance. An example is a spending plan or cash-flow forecast that can be used for measuring disbursements.

COST CONTROL

Cost control involves identifying when changes have been made to the cost baseline and managing those changes. In addition, cost control includes monitoring factors that cause changes to the cost baseline, as well as influencing those changes so that they are beneficial to the project.

Cost control is heavily related to other project variables and should be considered in conjunction with other control components, such as schedule control. For example, making changes based on cost variances can result in changes to the project schedule. Inappropriate responses to cost variances can cause quality or schedule problems or produce an unacceptable level of risk later in the project. An important part of cost control is to determine what is causing the variance and to decide whether the variance requires corrective action.

EARNED VALUE MANAGEMENT (EVM)

Comparing planned cash flow with actual cash flow has its uses, but it does not tell you whether the project will be over or under budget. To get the true picture of cost performance, the planned and actual costs for all completed tasks need to be compared. This is accomplished with a technique called earned value management. Earned value management uses cost data to give more accurate cost and schedule reports. It does this by combining cost and schedule status to provide a complete picture of the project. For example, projects can be ahead of schedule (good) but over budget (bad). Alternatively, they can be ahead of schedule (good) and under budget (good).

All EVM control account plans must continuously measure project performance by relating three independent values: the planned value, the earned value, and the actual costs incurred

Question	Answer	Acronym
How much should be done?	Planned Value	PV
How much work is done? This is the actual earned value of the project, because it is the value of the work that has been completed.	Earned Value	EV
How much work did the "is done" work cost?	Actual Cost	AC
What was the total job supposed to cost?	Budget at Completion	BAC
What do we now expect the total job to cost? This is a reestimate of the total project budget. It's a way of saying that if current cost performance trends continue, the final cost can be predicted.	Estimate at completion	EAC

Planned value (PV) = portion of approved cost estimate planned to be spent on the activity in a given period.

Actual cost (AC) = total of costs incurred in accomplishing work on the activity during a given period.

Earned value (EV) = value of work actually completed.

Interpretation of EV: "Task A, which I was supposed to complete today, is scheduled to cost $1,000. I have completed only 85 percent of this task. Thus, I have completed $850 worth of work, which is my earned value (EV)."

COST VARIANCE (CV)

Recalculating the estimated cost at completion using earned value implies that current trends will continue. Nevertheless, be careful not to assume that just because you are over budget now, you will be granted more money for your budget. Instead, the cost variance (CV) should be used as a warning flag to help you identify problems early, when there is still time to get back on track.

Cost variance (CV) = EV - AC
CV = BCWP - ACWP

Interpretation of CV: "I have done $850 worth of work (EV), but it actually cost me $900 to do this (AC). It has cost me $50 more to do what I have done than I originally thought (CV)."

SCHEDULE VARIANCE (SV)

Is the project on schedule? This is a question that all stakeholders want answered. However, it can be difficult to measure the degree to which a project is ahead or behind schedule. What if the majority of tasks are on schedule, but a few are ahead of schedule and others are behind? What is the accurate description of this project's schedule status? In this kind of situation, earned calculations can help measure schedule variances (SV) just as they help measure cost variances (CV).

Using the cost figures as the basis for schedule measurement is useful because it takes into account the number and size of tasks that are behind schedule. In other words, if ten concurrent tasks, each worth $25,000, are all one week behind schedule, the scheduled variances will be larger than if only one of those tasks is one week behind schedule.

Schedule variance (SV) = EV - PV

Interpretation of SV: "As of today, I was supposed to have done $1,000 worth of work on Task A (PV). I have actually done $850 worth of work (EV). Thus, I am behind in my schedule by $150 worth of work (SV)."

The formulas for cost variance (CV) and schedule variance (SV) will yield either a positive or negative numeric value. If the value is positive, then the project is under budget and ahead of schedule; if negative, then the project is over budget and behind schedule.

It is common to have a negative cost variance (i.e., to be over budget) and to have a positive schedule variance. This means that although you have overspent at that point, you are ahead of schedule. So the project is not necessarily in trouble. It may mean that you were able to begin some tasks sooner than planned.

COST PERFORMANCE INDEX (CPI)

CPI is the relationship between actual costs expended and the value of the physical work performed and is widely used as a forecasting tool because it is very accurate. Once a project is roughly 20 percent complete, the total CPI for a project generally does not change by more than 10 percent. Therefore, CPI gives the project team and stakeholders a quick and reliable estimate of final project costs.

CPI = EV ÷ AC or
CPI = BCWP ÷ ACWP

Interpretation of CPI: "I have done $850 worth of work (EV). It has cost me $900 to do so (AC). Each dollar I actually spent generated 94.4 cents worth of work (cost performance factor)."

SCHEDULE PERFORMANCE INDEX (SPI)

SPI is the relationship between the value of the initial planned schedule and the value of the physical work to be performed.

SPI = EV ÷ PV or
SPI = BCWP ÷ BCWS

Interpretation of SPI: "I have done $1,500 worth of work (EV). The value of work scheduled is $1,000. Each dollar of scheduled work generated $1.50 worth of work (schedule performance factor).

To interpret CPI and SPI: if they are equal to 1, then the project is on budget and schedule; if the equation equals less than 1, then the project is over budget and behind schedule; if the equation is greater than 1, then the project is under budget and ahead of schedule.

CPI and SPI provide the same information as CV and SV whether the project is on budget and schedule – but in a decimal format. For instance a CPI of 0.85 means that for every dollar spent, you have generated 85 cents of worth or work. This is a much more meaningful measure and is very good for use in status reports.

ESTIMATE TO COMPLETE (ETC)

The estimate to complete (ETC) is the amount of money needed to fund the project to completion.

ETC = EAC - AC or
ETC = EAC - ACWP

The estimate to complete (ETC) is a useful calculation because it tells the project manager how much money will be needed to complete the project. It is especially useful within small companies because it provides an estimate of cash-flow requirements for the project's remaining life.

ESTIMATE AT COMPLETION (EAC)

What do we now expect the total job to cost? The EAC is a forecast of most likely total project costs based on project performance and quantitative risk analysis. The PMBOK Guide provides three formulas for computing EAC:

Formula	When Used
EAC = AC + (Remaining PV ÷ CPI)	Use when current variances are seen as typical of future variances
EAC = AC + ETC	Use when past performance shows original estimates were fundamentally flawed or are no longer relevant because of a change in conditions
EAC = AC + Remaining AC	Use when current variances are seen as a typical

Another formula that may appear on the exam, and is not included in the PMBOK Guide, is:

EAC = BAC ÷ CPI

VARIANCE AT COMPLETION (VAC)

- Compares what the total job is supposed to cost - Budget at Completion (BAC)
- To what the total job is expected to cost - Estimate at Completion (EAC)
- Gives Variance at Completion (VAC)
- BAC - EAC = VAC

BAC AND VAC

Budget at completion, or BAC, is the estimated total cost of the project finished, which is generally calculated before a project begins. The BAC is calculated by assigning together all individual BCWS calculations for each portion of a project. Another name for BAC is the "baseline."

Variance at completion, or VAC, indicates a deviation from the budget at completion, which was projected before the project began. When finding the estimate at completion, or the total estimated cost for a project once the project is partially complete, you should determine the VAC using the following equation:

$$VAC = BAC - EAC$$

Determining the VAC helps indicate any significant cost variances that should be reported to project stakeholders. If the variance is great enough, the project manager should consult the team's cost management plan in order to take the correct cost control measures.

THE 50-50 RULE OF PROGRESS REPORTING

The 50-50 rule was established to overcome the problem of making subjective estimates (for example, estimating how far along we are on a task).

When beginning a task, charge 50 percent of its PV to its account. When the task is finally completed, charge the remaining 50 percent to its account.

Variations of the 50-50 Rule

- 20 - 80 rule: More conservative
- 0 - 100 rule: Most conservative. The assumption here is that a task does not have value until it is completed.

REVISED COST ESTIMATES

These are adjustment and/or updates to the cost information portion of the project. They differ from budget updates, which are a special category of revised cost estimates. Budget updates are changes to an approved cost baseline and generally are revised only in response to scope changes. In some cases, cost variances may be so severe that re-baselining is required to provide a realistic measure of performance.

Specifically with this section you need to be comfortable with the following three components:

- Budget cost of work performed (BCWP): How much is the work that has been worth? How much money was planned to spend on the work that has been done so far?
- Budgeted cost of work scheduled (BCWS): What is the budget that was set aside as of today or up to this point in time – the budgeted cost for the work scheduled as of today?
- Actual cost of work performed (ACWP): What is the actual cost of the work performed? How much has been spent for the work that has been accomplished.

CHAPTER REVIEW

1. If the work to date on a project were estimated to cost $1,500 and finish today, but, instead, cost $1,350 and is only two-thirds complete, what is the cost variance?
    A. -$150
    B. -$500
    C. -$350
    D. +$150

2. Which of the following calculations can't be used to determine EAC?
    A. AC to date plus a new estimate for all remaining work
    B. EV to date plus the remaining project budget
    C. AC to date plus the remaining budget modified by a performance factor
    D. AC to date plus the remaining budget

3. You are working on a construction project and just realize that cost budgeting is important because the budget is used to measure and monitor project cost performance. Overall, cost estimates must be allocated to individual activities or work packages to establish the project cost baseline. In an ideal situation, a project manager would prefer to prepare estimates:
    A. After the budget is approved
    B. Using a bottom-up estimating method
    C. Using a parametric model
    D. Before the budget request

4. The time-phased budget that will be used to measure and monitor cost performance in the project is called the:
    A. Project schedule
    B. Cost budget baseline
    C. Cost baseline
    D. Work breakdown structure

5. _____ is the sum of the budgets for work accomplished in a given time period.
    A. Budgeted cost of work performed earned value
    B. Actual cost of work performed actual costs
    C. Budgeted cost of work scheduled planned value.
    D. Budget at completion

6. If the cost variance is the same as the schedule variance and both numbers are greater than zero, then:
    A. The cost variance is due to the schedule variance
    B. The variance is favorable to the project
    C. The schedule variance can be easily corrected
    D. Labor rates have escalated since the project began

7. As a project manager, you are allocating project costs relating to training and training materials. This type of expense should be considered:
    A. Direct cost
    B. Hidden cost
    C. Sunk cost
    D. Indirect cost

8. All of the following are examples of tools often used in cost estimating except:
    A. Parametric modeling
    B. Duration estimating
    C. Bottom-up estimating
    D. Analogous estimating

9. You are currently working on a project and you have just completed a review of cost performance data. Different responses will be required depending on the degree of variance from the baseline. For example, a variance of 10 percent might not require immediate action, whereas a variance of 100 percent will require investigation. A description of how you plan to manage cost variances should be included in the:
    A. Change management plan
    B. Variance management plan
    C. Performance measurement plan
    D. Cost management plan

10. Based upon your readings, the cumulative CPI has been shown to be relatively stable after what percentage of project completion?
    A. 15 to 20 percent
    B. 5 to 10 percent
    C. 50 to 75 percent
    D. 25 to 35 percent

11. You have been working with the benefits and compensation committee for ten months and finally your company has established a reward and recognition system for its project management professionals. Project cost performance is used as a criterion to determine rewards. What should you do to ensure that rewards reflect actual performance?
    A. Prepare a cost baseline
    B. Consider overtime work as part of the job
    C. Estimate and budget controllable and uncontrollable costs separately
    D. Use earned value management to monitor performance

12. You are currently working on an IT project and need to assign costs to the time period in which they are incurred. To do this, you should:
    A. Use the project schedule as an input to cost budgeting
    B. Identify the project components so that costs can be allocated
    C. Prepare a cost performance plan
    D. Prepare a detailed and accurate cost estimate

13. _____ is another term for top-down estimating.
    A. Analogous estimating
    B. Life-cycle costing
    C. Parametric modeling
    D. Bottom-up estimating

14. Your approved cost baseline has changed because of a major scope change on your project. Your next step should be to?
    A. Issue a budget update
    B. Update the work breakdown structure to adjust for a new period
    C. Implement the scope management plan
    D. Review previous lessons learned

15. A project was estimated to cost $1.5 million and scheduled to last six months. After three months, the earned value analysis shows the following: EV = $650,000, PV = $750,000, and AC = $800,000. The schedule and cost variances are:
    A. SV = -$100,000 ÷ CV = -$150,000
    B. SV = -$50,000 ÷ CV = +$150,000
    C. SV = +$100,000 ÷ CV = +150,000
    D. SV = +150,000 ÷ CV = -$100,000

16. Which of the following is a tool for analyzing a design, determining its functions, and assessing how to provide those functions cost effectively?
    A. Cost break-even analysis
    B. Value added analysis
    C. Configuration management
    D. Value engineering

17. You are managing an e-business project for your firm and a partner in charge is obsessed with earning as much profit as possible to increase revenue and ultimately his bonus. He keeps asking you for the profit "numbers." Which of the following categories of profit is he really interested in?
    A. Expected
    B. Operating
    C. Cumulative
    D. Gross

18. Inputs to cost budgeting include all of the following except?
    A. Cost estimates
    B. Project schedule
    C. Work breakdown structure
    D. Cost baseline

19. According to PMI, the method of calculating the EAC by adding the remaining project budget to the actuals to date is used most often when the?
    A. Original estimating assumptions are no longer reliable because conditions have changed
    B. Current variances are viewed as atypical ones
    C. Original estimating assumptions are considered to be fundamentally flawed
    D. Current variances are viewed as typical of future variances

20. Which is a phased budget used to measure and monitor cost performance on the project?
    A. Cost baseline
    B. Project schedule
    C. Cost management plan
    D. EAC

ANSWERS

1. C
2. B
3. D
4. C
5. A
6. B
7. A
8. B
9. D
10. A
11. C
12. A
13. A
14. A
15. A
16. D
17. B
18. D
19. D
20. A

PROJECT QUALITY MANAGEMENT

7

The Project Quality Management questions on the PMP exam are straightforward. The exam is likely to reflect the current emphasis on customer satisfaction and continuous improvement through quality tools such as Pareto analysis and cause-and-effect diagrams. You must know the difference among quality planning, quality assurance, and quality control.

PMBOK Guide includes all quality-related activities under the term Project Quality Management, which compromise the three quality processes mentioned above. Review PMBOK Guide figure 8.1 for an overview of the Project Quality Management structure.

The Project Quality Management knowledge area assures that the project meets the requirements that the project was undertaken to produce. These processes measure overall performance, monitor the project's results, and compare them to the quality standards set out in the project planning process to assure that the customer will receive the product or service they thought they purchased.

Project Quality Management is composed of the following three processes:

- Quality Planning: involves defining quality standards and deciding how to achieve them.
- Quality Assurance: consists of measuring project progress to ensure the product meets quality standards.
- Quality Control: involves supervising project activity completion and correcting any errors.

The purpose of quality management during the project management process is to identify customers' needs, to develop goals based on those needs, and to identify factors that impede achievement of project goals. Another aim of quality management is to keep a project on schedule, which helps avoid sacrificing quality in the interest of time and cost.

Before beginning a project, it is important for you the project manager to have a solid understanding of quality management and how its components are integrated into the project management process. The components of quality management fit into these steps of the project management process:

- Quality planning is part of the planning step of the project management process.
- Quality improvement is part of the executing step of the project management process.
- Quality control is part of the controlling step of the project management process.

The PMBOK Guide defines quality as the totality of characteristics of an entity that bears on its ability to satisfy stated or implied needs.

Stated and implied needs are the inputs to developing project requirements. A critical aspect of quality management in the project context is turning implied needs into requirements through Project Scope Management.

It is important to recognize the difference between quality and grade. Grade is defined by the PMBOK Guide as a category or rank given to entities having the same functional use but different technical characteristics. Low quality is always a problem, but low grade may not be. The project manager and team must determine and deliver the required levels of quality and grade.

One important area that is emphasized in the PMBOK Guide is the growing attention to customer requirements as the basis for managing quality. Much of this discussion is similar to what is covered in contemporary course offerings.

Another concept that may appear on the test, which is not specifically mentioned in the PMBOK Guide, is "gold-plating." Simply defined, gold-plating gives the customer more than what was required. Exceeding the specified requirements is a waste of time and money, with no value added to the project. The customer should expect and receive exactly what was specified. This is the underlying philosophy of project quality management espoused by PMI; it is the process required to ensure that the project will satisfy the needs for which it was undertaken.

QUALITY MANAGEMENT

The PMBOK Guide definition is similar to Philip Crosby's definition in *Quality is Free* (Mass Market Paerbacks, 1979). Quality management includes all activities of the overall management function that determine the quality policy, objectives, and responsibilities, and implements them by means such as quality planning, quality assurance, quality control, and quality improvement within the quality system. Quality management involves carrying out a project through its phases (for example, concept, development, implementation, and finish) with zero deviations from the project specifications. Policies, plans, procedures, specifications, and requirements are attained through the subfunctions of quality assurance and quality control.

PIONEERS OF QUALITY MANAGEMENT

Traditional quality performance standards were based on the assumption that defects and errors are inevitable. The following pioneers of quality management practices believed that defects and errors could be predicted and eliminated before taking root:

DR. W. EDWARDS DEMING

Dr. Deming theorized that when correcting problems, managers made changes to a project 85 percent of the time, and that 15 percent of the problems that occurred were errors that team members could fix or avoid. The Deming Cycle for Improvement calls for project planning, team member training, efficient activity execution, verification that activities meet project goals, and documentation of lessons learned.

DR. JOSEPH M. JURAN

Dr. Juran developed what is called the Juran Trilogy, which emphasizes quality improvement, quality planning, and quality control. In addition to this trilogy, Dr. Juran is known for his Ten Steps to Quality Improvement. He recognized the importance of products being fit for customers' use and was concerned with the legal side of quality standards.

PHILLIP B. CROSBY

Phillip Crosby assembled what he called the 14 Steps to Quality Improvement. He also developed Four Absolutes of Quality: a product must measure up to all requirements, error prevention is key to high quality, all projects should strive for "zero defects," and activities should be done correctly the first time.

AWARDS FOR QUALITY MANAGEMENT PRACTICES

Awards for quality management are incentives for companies to excel at providing quality products and services. Awards, sometimes created by government agencies, encourage companies to implement strict quality standards. Two awards for exceptional quality management practices include:

THE MALCOLM BALDRIGE NATIONAL QUALITY AWARD

The Malcolm Baldrige National Quality Award, which was established with the Malcolm Baldrige National Quality Improvement Act of 1987. This Act promotes company knowledge of quality management practices, and the award recognizes quality-related accomplishments. Criteria for this award include leadership, planning strategies, resource management, and customer satisfaction.

THE DEMING AWARD

The Deming Award was established by the Union of Japanese Scientists and Engineers. The Union of Japanese Scientists and Engineers bestow the Deming Award based on such things as a company's quality and management policy, organization, policy implementation, and problem-solving capabilities.

Companies can use the standards for the Malcolm Baldrige and Deming Awards to develop organizational and quality policies or to measure the performance of their current quality policies.

QUALITY PLANNING

Quality planning involves defining the quality standards for a project and deciding how to achieve those standards. The scope statement is used as a point of reference during quality planning because it outlines not only the end results of a project, but also the project objectives, which should be in-line with the stakeholder expectations.

An important part of quality planning involves making sure quality is part of a product's design from the beginning of a project, since quality cannot be infused into a product through inspection. Remember that the result of the quality planning process is the quality plan. Also remember a fundamental principle from Deming is that "quality should be planned in, not inspected in."

Therefore, although inspection is certainly part of project quality management, increased inspection is not generally considered the best path to improved quality. So hiring more inspectors would not be the correct answer to the question, "What is the best way to improve quality?"

QUALITY POLICY

PMI stresses the importance of having a quality policy for the project. Quality policy is a company's statement of how it will produce quality products and what it will do if products are defective. Most often, upper management dictates a quality policy to be implemented by project managers and team members. Not all quality polices are formal documents. If a company does not have a formal quality policy, then the project managers and team members should draft one before starting a new project. It is important that a project's stakeholders know the terms of the quality policy before a project begins.

QUALITY PLANNING TOOLS AND TECHNIQUES

PMI discusses five quality planning tools and techniques.

BENEFIT/COST ANALYSIS

Benefit/cost analysis must be considered in the quality planning process. Benefit/cost analysis weighs the benefits versus cost to make sure a project meets quality requirements without going over the project's budget.

BENCHMARKING

Benchmarking compares planned project activities to past project activities. This technique allows the project manager to determine what adjustments should be made to the project before work begins. Some people have described this process as a search for "best practices."

FLOWCHARTING

Flowcharts, such as cause and effect diagrams, are used to illustrate relationships among each part of a project.

DESIGN OF EXPERIMENTS

This is an analytical technique that helps identify which variables have the most influence on the overall outcome. For example, designers might want to determine which combination of suspension and tires will produce the most desirable ride characteristics at a reasonable cost. Or, project planners could design experiments to determine the optimal combination of senior- and junior-level staff given cost and time constraints.

COST OF QUALITY

One major area of emphasis is the concept of cost of quality. Cost of quality refers to the amount of money and resources that are necessary to make sure a project's quality standards are met. It is defined as the cost of conformance (the cost of proactive quality processes) and the cost of nonconformance (the cost of a quality failure). In either form, cost of quality is a results-oriented approach to measuring and assessing the effectiveness and/or benefit of an organization's project quality management process. It is a useful means of bringing management's attention to the need for quality, but it provides little meaningful capability to manage quality proactively.

TYPES OF COSTS

There are two types of costs incurred in quality management. Be able to recognize examples of each: prevention costs and appraisal costs, which are the cost of conformance; and failure costs, which are the cost of nonconformance.

COST OF CONFORMANCE

Prevention costs: Up-front costs that are oriented toward the satisfaction of customer requirements:

- Design reviews
- Training and indoctrination
- Planning
- Vendor, supplier, and subcontractor surveys
- Process studies

Appraisal costs: Costs associated with the evaluation of the product or the process to see whether customer requirements were met:

- Product inspections
- Lab tests
- Vendor controls
- In-process testing
- Internal/external design reviews

COST OF NONCONFORMANCE (FAILURE COSTS)

Internal failure costs: Costs associated with the failure of the processes to make the products acceptable to the customer before the products leave the control of the organization:

- Scrap / Rework
- Repair
- Downtime
- Defect evaluation
- Corrective actions

External failure costs: Costs associated with the determination by the customer that requirements have not been satisfied:

- Customer returns
- Customer complaints
- Customer inspections
- Customer visits to resolve quality complaints
- Corrective actions

REWORK

Rework is the corrective action taken to make a defective product conform to a project's quality standards. Reworking a product takes more time and uses more resources than if the product is made correctly the first time. The use of additional time and resources increases the cost of quality, which is the total amount of money and work used to make quality products.

KEY QUALITY PLANNING OUTPUTS

The quality management plan describes the quality management system: the organizational structure, responsibilities, procedures, processes, and resources needed to implement quality management.

Operational definitions describe what something is and how the quality control process measures it. They may also be called metrics.

Checklists are outputs of quality planning that are used to verify that a set of required steps has been performed. Completed checklists (an output of quality control) should be part of the project's records.

QUALITY ASSURANCE

Quality assurance is a managerial function that addresses all the planned and systematic activities implemented within the quality system to provide confidence that the project will satisfy the relevant quality standards.

Quality assurance refers to project activities that are planned and executed to ensure quality products and services. The goal of quality assurance is the improved quality of a project's processes and improved quality of end products. Any problems encountered during the execution of quality assurance activities must be corrected. Correcting problems can lead to greater efficiency, decreased cost of production, and a higher-quality product.

Quality assurance is important not only because it leads to the correction of problems, but also because it gives customers and project stakeholder's confidence that the finished product will be free of defects.

The following issues and concepts fall under quality assurance:

FORMATIVE QUALITY EVALUATION (QUALITY AUDIT)
This is a process of reviewing specific data at key points of the project's life cycle. The quality audit is a quality assurance tool and technique that serves as a structured review of quality management activities. Its objective is to identify lessons learned that can be used to improve performance on this project or on other projects in the organization.

QUALITY IMPROVEMENT
Quality improvement is the output of quality assurance and includes taking actions to increase the effectiveness and efficiency of the project to provide an added benefit to the project stakeholders. This may require the use of change requests or corrective action.

OWNERSHIP OF QUALITY RESPONSIBILITY
The individual employee performing the task has ultimate responsibility.

SELF-INSPECTION
The individual performing a given task also performs measurements to ensure that conformance is continually achieved.

QUALITY CONTROL
Quality control is a technical function that involves establishing the technical baseline for the project and then collecting specific data by which to measure conformance to that baseline. Quality control measures are used throughout a project's life cycle to make sure work is done properly and that actual project results match the expectations outlined in the project's quality management plan. During quality control, both the processes used to complete the project, as well as the end product, are examined to make sure they meet quality standards.

The purpose of quality control is to ensure that a finished product has certain quality characteristics and that unacceptable product traits are corrected.

It is important to understand that quality control is not only a component of the quality management variable, but that it is also part of the fourth step of the project management process—project control.

The difference between quality control and quality assurance is that quality assurance focuses on developing and implementing quality-related activities, whereas quality control focuses on ensuring that the quality-related activities achieve their desired effect.

Quality control and quality assurance are similar in that both components use a project's quality management plan and operational definitions to evaluate whether or not a project and product are achieving the desired levels of quality. The quality control and quality assurance components are also similar in that both result in quality improvement.

Included below are some important terms and concepts associated with quality control.

- Variable: A quality characteristic that is measurable in increments. Examples are diameter measured in inches, cooking time measured in minutes, and weight measured in pounds.
- Attribute: A quality characteristic that is classified as either conforming or nonconforming to specifications or requirements. It results in a go or no-go decision.
- Probability. An important concept in quality control is that of probability. In its simplest form, probability refers to the chance that something will happen.

For attributes, this is easily segregated into a "yes-no" outcome. As an example, in flipping a coin there is a 50-percent probability of getting "heads" on any single flip.

For variables, probability is a more complicated concept. We measure the occurrences of an event or characteristic, and distribute them over the entire range of the characteristic. Such a distribution is formally called a probability distribution. The most common probability distribution has a bell shape and is symmetric about its mean; it is known as a normal distribution or a bell curve.

A population is the entire group of items or occurrences that we might wish to measure. Because populations can be very large, however, we often sample the population, using a smaller group to get a picture of the larger group.

Standard Deviation: In measuring samples and comparing them to their overall population, one important concept is that of standard deviation. Simply defined, the standard deviation is the amount on either side of the mean of a normal distribution that will contain approximately 68.3 percent of the total population. The amount within two standard deviations will include 95.5 percent, and within three standard deviations will include 99.7 percent of the population.

Calculating standard deviation is complex. Most automated quality control packages include the provision to calculate standard deviation and other statistically important values. In fact, most pocket calculators available today can also provide this value for a series of discrete observations of a variable characteristic.

Process Control: Building on the statistical concepts we have just discussed, the PMBOK Guide emphasizes process control as an important means of managing quality. Key to this concept is the idea of statistical process control (SPC) and its main tool—control charts—commonly called SPC charts.

A SPC chart will show you the current capability of the process—what is called voice of the process in some courses and recent publications. The important point to remember about SPC charts is that there are many different types you may use, depending on the characteristic you are measuring and its variability.

Sampling: Sampling is a useful means of assessing the value of a characteristic when examining an entire population is not feasible. There are two main types of sampling.

- **Attribute sampling** is the examination of one or more attributes in a lot. A limit of acceptability is established for the entire lot. For example, we may consider a "lot" of 10,000 parts. A random sample of 150 parts is selected for examination. For that sample, the acceptance number is 3, meaning that if more than 3 parts are found to be defective; the entire lot of 10,000 will be rejected. You can conduct single-attribute sampling, double-attribute sampling, multiple-attribute sampling, or sequential attribute sampling (single-attribute sampling performed sequentially on the same lot for different attributes).
- **Variable sampling** provides a more dynamic approach to sampling. This is the basis for creating control charts, where a process variable is measured and charted to determine process capability. Variable sampling may also be used to estimate the fraction of a lot that is nonconforming, and thus to make decisions about further inspection or use of the lot.

Both attribute sampling and variation sampling tell whether a product does or does not conform to quality standards. However, variation sampling also accounts for the degree to which a product does or does not conform.

PREVENTION AND INSPECTION

Prevention and inspection have different purposes. Prevention requires careful planning to avoid errors before a project begins. Inspection occurs during project execution or after a project is completed. When defects are found during inspection, rework is required to correct the defects before products are distributed to customers.

SPECIAL CAUSES AND RANDOM CAUSES

Special causes of variation, which are often caused by human error, are generally unexpected or unanticipated. Random causes, also called common causes, of variation are normal difficulties associated with a certain process, such as equipment failure or faulty product design. Project team members who contribute to special causes of variation should be able to correct the causes on their own, whereas project managers are responsible for solving random causes of variation since the causes are part of the project's process.

TOLERANCE AND CONTROL LIMITS

Tolerance refers to the amount off acceptable variations from product quality standards. Control limits apply to a project's process rather than to a product. A project is considered "in control" if its processes are within specified control limits.

STATISTICAL QUALITY CONTROL

Statistical quality control is used to evaluate the extent of product variation and to identify what changes, if any, must be made to production processes in order to decrease product variation. Data points on a graph represent incidents of product variations, and a normal distribution curve indicates whether or not the variations are of a degree acceptable for quality standards.

Quality monitoring involves the use of statistics. Therefore, it is important to know the following basic statistical terms:

- **Population** – refers to the total number of product units produced during a project.
- **Sample size** – refers to the number of product units taken from the population for evaluation during a project's quality monitoring process. This number varies depending on the product, the time of the inspection, and a company's needs.
- **Mean** – this refers to the sum of the sample divided by the number of units in the sample. For example, in the sample {2, 4, 6, 8}, the mean is (2 + 4 + 6 + 8) ÷ 4. The mean is 5.
- **Median** – When an odd—numbered set of data is arranged sequentially, the middle number in the set is the median. For example, in the set {3, 6, 9}, the median is 6. When an even-numbered set of data is arranged sequentially, the median is the average of the middle two numbers. For example, in the set {2, 4, 8, 9}, the median is (4 + 8) ÷ 2, the median is 6.
- **Mode** – In a sample of data, the number that occurs most frequently represents the mode. For example, in the set {2, 3, 4, 3, 5, 3, 4}, the mode is 3.

QUALITY CONTROL TOOLS

There are seven main quality control tools (often called the basic seven tools), which are illustrated and discussed below.

FLOWCHARTS AND DIAGRAMS

Flowcharts permit you to examine and understand relationships in a process or project. They show how various elements of a system interrelate. They provide a step-by-step schematic, or picture, that serves to create a common language, ensure common understanding about sequence, and focus collective attention on shared concerns. Flowcharts are used in all three of the quality management processes. Several different types of flowcharts are particularly useful in the continuous improvement process. Three frequently used charts are known as the top-down flowchart, the detailed flowchart, and the work-flow diagram.

The top-down flowchart presents only the major or most fundamental steps in a process or project. It helps you or your team to easily visualize the process in a single, simple flow diagram. Key value-added actions associated with each major activity are listed below their respective flow diagram steps. You can construct a top-down flowchart fairly quickly and easily. You generally do so before attempting to produce detailed flowcharts for a process. By limiting the top-down flowchart to a value-added activity, the likelihood of becoming bogged down in detail is signifactly reduced.

The detailed flowchart provides very specific information about process flow. At its most detailed level, every decision point, feedback loop, and process step is represented. Detailed flowcharts should be used only when the level of detail provided by the top-down or other simpler flowcharts is insufficient to support understanding, analysis, and improvement activity. The detailed flowchart may also be useful and appropriate for critical processes where precisely following a specific procedure is essential.

The work-flow diagram is a graphic representation of how work actually flows through a physical space or facility. It is very useful for analyzing flow processes, illustrating flow inefficiency, and planning process flow improvement.

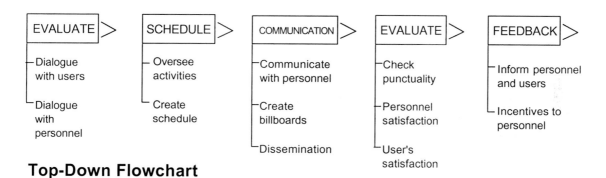

Top-Down Flowchart

SCATTER DIAGRAMS
Scatter diagrams are used to investigate the possible relationship between two variables that both relate to the same "event." A straight line of best fit (using the least squares method) is often included. Things to look for:

- If the points cluster in a band running from lower left to upper right, there is a positive correlation (if x increases, y increases).
- If the points cluster in a band from upper left to lower right, there is a negative correlation (if x increases, y decreases).
- Imagine drawing a straight line or curve through the data so that it "fits" as well as possible. The more the points cluster closely around the imaginary line of best fit, the stronger the relationship that exists between the two variables.

- If it is hard to see where you would draw a line, and if the points show no significant clustering, there is probably no correlation.

NOTE: There is a maxim in statistics that says, "Correlation does not imply causality." In other words, your scatter plot may show that a relationship exists, but it does not and cannot prove that one variable is causing the other. There could be a third factor involved that is causing both, some other systemic cause, or the apparent relationship could just be a fluke. Nevertheless, the scatter plot can give you a clue that two things might be related, and if so, how they move together.

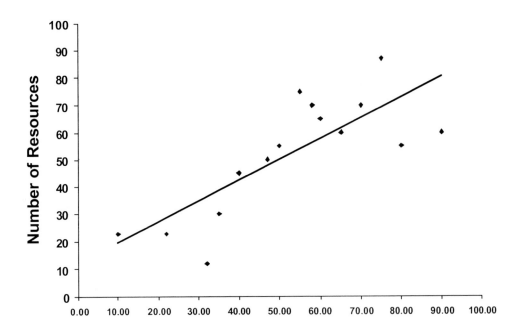

PARETO CHARTS

In the late 1800s, Vilfredo Pareto, an Italian economist, found that typically 80 percent of the wealth in a region was concentrated in less than 20 percent of the population. Later, Dr. Joseph Juran formulated what he called the Pareto Principle of Problems: only a "vital few" elements (20 percent) account for the majority (80 percent) of the problems. For example, in a manufacturing facility, 20 percent of the equipment problems account for 80 percent of the downtime. Because the Pareto Principle has proven to be valid in numerous situations, it is useful to examine data carefully to identify the vital few items that most deserve attention.

A Pareto Chart is a bar chart in which the data are arranged in descending order of their importance, generally by magnitude of frequency, cost, time, or a similar parameter. The chart presents the information being examined in its order of priority and focuses attention on the most critical issues. The chart aids the decision-making process because it puts issues into an easily understood framework in which relationships and relative contributions are clearly evident.

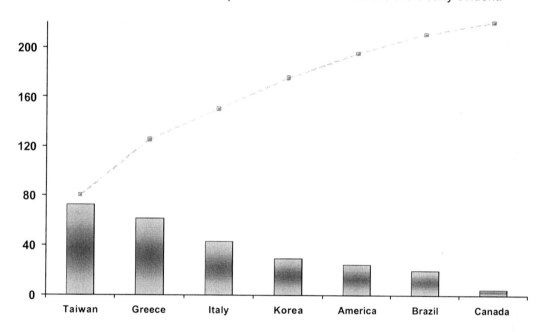

CAUSE-AND-EFFECT DIAGRAM

Cause-and-effect diagrams are the brainchild of Kaoru Ishikawa, who pioneered quality management processes in the Kawasaki shipyards, in Japan, and in the process became one of the founding fathers of modern management. The cause-and-effect diagram is used to explore all the potential or real causes (or inputs) that result in a single effect (or output). Causes are arranged according to their level of importance or detail, resulting in a depiction of relationships and hierarchy of events. This can help you search for root causes, identify areas where there may be problems, and compare the relative importance of different causes.

Causes in a cause-and-effect diagram are frequently arranged into four major categories. While these categories can be anything, you will often see: manpower, methods, materials, and machinery (recommended for manufacturing) equipment, policies, procedures, and people (recommended for administration and service). These guidelines can be helpful but should not be used if they limit the diagram or are inappropriate. The categories you use should suit your needs.

The cause-and-effect diagram is also known as the fishbone diagram because it was drawn to resemble the skeleton of a fish, with the main causal categories drawn as "bones" attached to the spine of the fish, as shown on the next page.

Cause-and-effect diagrams can also be drawn as tree diagrams, resembling a tree turned on its side. From a single outcome or trunk, branches extend that represent major categories of inputs or causes that create that single outcome. These large branches then lead to smaller and smaller branches of causes all the way down to twigs at the ends. The tree structure has an advantage over the fishbone-style diagram. As a fishbone diagram becomes more and more complex, it becomes difficult to find and compare items that are the same distance from the effect because they are dispersed over the diagram. With the tree structure, all items on the same causal level are aligned vertically.

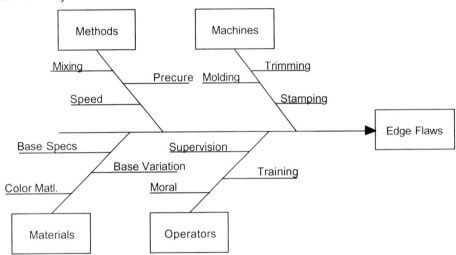

GRAPHS

Many different types of graphs are available and useful to the improvement process. Some of the most common include a simple line graph (time plots or trend chart), pie chart, and bar chart, or histogram. Graphs are useful for presenting data in a simple pictorial form that is quickly and easily understood. Graphs serve as powerful communication tools and should be employed liberally in the workplace to describe performance, support analyses, and document the improvement process.

CONTROL CHARTS

A control chart is a graph that displays data taken over time and computed variations of those data. Control charts are used to show the variation on a variety of variables including average (X) and range (R) and also the number of defects (PN), percent defective (P), defects per variable unit (U), and defects per fixed unit (C). The control chart allows you to distinguish between measurements that are predictably within the inherent capability of the process (normal causes of variation that are to be expected) and measurements that are unpredictable and produced by special causes.

The upper and lower control limits (UCL and LCL) must not be confused with specification limits. Control limits describe the natural variation of the process such that points within the limits are generally indicative of normal and expected variation. Points outside the limits signal that something has occurred that requires special attention because it is outside of the built-in systemic causes of variation in the process. Note that the circled point on the X-bar chart means that the process is out of control and should be investigated. These points outside the control limits are referred to as special events having either assignable causes or random causes.

The occurrence of assignable causes may be the result of unwanted, external effects such as the following:

- An equipment problem
- An employee problem (poor training, understaffed, and so on)
- Defective materials

There is another important guideline, known as the Rule of Seven, which should be observed whenever interpreting control charts. This rule of thumb (heuristic) states that if seven or more observations in a row occur on the same side of the mean (or if they trend in the same direction), even though they may be within the control limit, they should be investigated as if they had an assignable cause. It is extremely unlikely that seven observations in a row would be on the same side of the mean if the process is operating normally.

Why is this so? If a process is operating normally, the observations will follow a random pattern with some of the points falling above the line and some below the line. In fact, the probability that any single point will fall above or below the line is 50-50 (like a coin toss). Further, the probability that seven points in a row would be on the same side of the line would be calculated as 0.5 to the 7seventh power, which is equal to 0.0078 (or less than 1 percent). Again, this rule provides a guideline that alerts you that something unlikely is happening and you should check it out.

These charts will help you understand the following:

- The inherent capability of your processes
- Bring your processes under control by eliminating the special causes of variation
- Reduce tampering with processes that are under statistical control
- Monitor the effects of process changes aimed at improvement

Two additional concepts are important in the use of control charts. Both concepts involve the idea of standard deviation, often referred to as "sigma." For the exam, you need to understand only the concepts (no formulas or complex calculations are required).

The first concept involves the use by some companies of what is known as the Six Sigma Rule for setting control limits. You are already aware that three standard deviations (sigma) either side of the mean accounts for approximately 99.7 percent of the possible outcomes. Historically, many companies have used plus or minus three sigmas as their standard for setting control limits. In recent years, some companies have chosen to use plus or minus six sigmas as a guide for setting control limits. The use of this more stringent rule means that even fewer actual outcomes might fall outside the control limits.

The second concept involves the effect of sample size on the control limits. Again, you do not need to memorize any formulas, but it helps to know the following information about how the formula for setting control limits works. First, the standard deviation is part of the formula for establishing control limits. The larger the standard deviation, the wider the control limits will be. That much is fairly intuitive. In other words, the greater the natural variations in the process, the wider the control limits need to be. Now, how does sample size affect the control limits? Sample size affects control limits by its effect on the standard deviation. Sample size is in the denominator of the formula for variance from which standard deviation is computed; so whenever sample size is increased, the standard deviation will be smaller. Conversely, if the sample size is decreased, the standard deviation will be larger. Therefore, larger sample sizes will result in more narrow control limits, and smaller sample sizes will result in wider control limits.

CHECKSHEETS
A checksheet is a list of check-off items that permit data to be collected quickly and easily in a simple standardized format that lends itself to quantitative analysis. A checksheet frequently contains a graphic representation of an object and is used to record such information as where specific damage was located. A checksheet is intended to make data collection fast and easy and it should be carefully designed so that the data are useful and have a clear purpose. Checksheets are frequently used to collect data on numbers of defective items, defect locations, and defect causes.

CONTINUOUS IMPROVEMENT AND KAIZEN
Kaizen, was originally defined in the book *Kaizen, the Key to Japan's Competitive Success*, by Mr. Masaaki Imai. Kaizen means improvement. Moreover, Kaizen means continuing improvement in personal life, home life, social life, and working life. When applied to the workplace Kaizen means continuing improvement involving everyone—managers and workers alike.

Kaizen is a Japanese word meaning gradual and orderly, continuous improvement. The Kaizen business strategy involves everyone in an organization working together to make improvements "without large capital investments."

Kaizen is a culture of sustained continuous improvement focusing on eliminating waste in all systems and processes of an organization. The Kaizen strategy begins and ends with people. With Kaizen, an involved leadership guides people to continuously improve their ability to meet expectations of high quality, low cost, and on-time delivery. Kaizen transforms companies into "Superior Global Competitors."

There are two elements that construct Kaizen: improvement and change for the better, and ongoing/continuity. Lacking one of those elements would not be considered Kaizen. For instance, the expression of "business as usual" contains the element of continuity without improvement. On the other hand, the expression of "breakthrough" contains the element of change or improvement without continuity. Kaizen should contain both elements.

Kaizen, as you could learn from the definition, is a common word and very natural to individual, continuous improvement in personal life, home life, social life, and work life. Everybody deserves to and should be willing to improve himself/herself for the better, continually. "If a man has not been seen for three days, his friends should take a good look at him to see what changes have befallen him," quoted from the old Japanese saying, describes how natural Kaizen is.

In our concepts, three functions should happen simultaneously within any organizations: maintenance, innovation, and Kaizen. By maintenance, we refer to maintaining the current status, the procedures are set, and the standards are implemented. This is generally the role of the people in the lower level of organizations—maintaining the company's standards.

Innovation refers to breakthrough activities initiated by top management: buying new machines, new equipment, developing new markets, directing research and design (R & D) , change of strategy, etc....

In the middle, there is Kaizen: small steps, but continuing improvement. The lower/middle management and the workers, with the encouragement and direction of the top, should implement Kaizen. The top management responsibility is to cultivate a Kaizen working climate and culture in the organization.

NOTE: For the PMP exam know that Kaizen is small, tiny, incremental improvements—always looking for a way to make things better.

JUST-IN-TIME (JIT)

Just-in-time is an inventory control approach process that continuously stresses waste reduction by optimizing the processes and procedures necessary to maintain an operation. Part of this process is JIT inventory where the materials needed appear just in time for use, thus eliminating costs associated with material handling and storage. The philosophy is that with no safety stock in the system, defective parts or processes will grind the system to a halt. A zero working-process inventory forces a company to find and fix quality problems, or it will constantly miss its schedule commitments.

The company benefits from JIT inventory/purchasing by developing long-term relationships with fewer suppliers, thus lowering subcontractor management costs. The contractor benefits by having long-term contracts.

Numerous companies in Japan have adopted JIT, because they believe JIT and high quality go together naturally, but in the United States it has only been marginally successful.

NOTE: Just-in-time (JIT) is designed as a process that is going to keep flow coming to you, as a vendor, just in time to prepare it, process it, and get it to your customers. Vendors do not want to keep inventory on hand. They do not want to have material in a warehouse. Classic just-in-time management allows for the flow of materials effectively through an organization or process.

IMPACT OF MOTIVATION ON QUALITY

It is generally believed that increased quality is likely to be associated with projects whose team members display pride, commitment, and an interest in workmanship. It is also believed that one way to harm this culture is by allowing frequent turnover of the people assigned to the project.

PRIORITY OF QUALITY VERSUS COST AND SCHEDULE

Quality use to receive lip service in many companies, but it was, in reality, less important than meeting schedules or containing costs. Such a situation was often tipped off by such signals as the quality manager reporting to the production manager (who often cared more about schedule pressures than quality). Although lip service has probably not been eliminated entirely, modern thinking emphasizes that quality should share equal priority with cost and schedule.

Philip Crosby titled his book *Quality is Free* on the premise that the cost of doing things twice is far greater than the cost of doing them right in the first time. When performance is cut, costs go up for many reasons, including these:

- Rework (performing the same tasks twice because they were not done right the first time) during the project will drive costs higher and delay completion.
- Rework after the project finishes is even more expensive than rework during the project. Any potential development cost savings are wiped out by the high cost of fixing the product.
- Failure due to poor product performance can also be expensive. Product recalls always bear the expense of contacting the consumers as well as fixing or replacing the product. Product failures such as collapsing bridges and malfunctioning medical equipment can even cost lives.
- Poor product performance causes damage to the reputation of the firm and ultimately reduces the demand for its products or services.

NOTE: The above paragraphs are very important because they drive home the point that sometimes, in some quality practices, what you are doing in the real world may not really matter. This is one of them. The argument in most quality circles is that quality is of equal importance to cost and schedule. In some circles, it is even said that quality is more important than cost or schedule. Nevertheless, for the PMP exam, you need to know that quality is of equal importance to cost and schedule. You need to know, if asked, what is more important, quality, cost, or schedule? The answer: they are equally important.

IMPACT OF POOR QUALITY

The following effects on a project are possible results of poor quality:

- Increased project costs as a result of costs of nonconformance (for example, rework, scrap, product recalls, and so on)
- Decreased productivity
- Increased risk and uncertainty (less predictability in cost, schedule, and technical outcomes)
- Increased costs of monitoring (if conformance to specifications is low, increased monitoring will probably become necessary)

NOTE: What happens when we do not have good quality? Look at the bullet points and memorize each and everyone of them. They are listed as bullets in order to make it easier to remember. Poor quality results in higher costs, poor productivity, increased risk, and increased uncertainty.

INSPECTIONS

Quality cannot be infused into a project or a product by inspection. However, inspection is a useful tool for quality control. End products should always go through a final inspection to make sure that they conform to quality standards. Another name for inspection is "walk-through."

TREND ANALYSIS

Trend analysis uses scatter diagrams to monitor the performance of technical operations, project costs, and a project's schedule. During trend analysis, a project manager determines the mathematical equation that best fits the slope of the line on a scatter diagram. The equation is then used to predict how changing one project variable will affect another project variable.

DESIGN AND QUALITY

Quality should be designed into, not inspected into (worth repeating). More specifically, careful design of a product or service is believed to increase reliability and maintainability (two important measures of quality).

The primary responsibility for developing design and test specifications rests with the project engineers (they have the expertise needed to perform this vital task).

Rework is any action taken to bring a defective or nonconforming item into compliance with requirements or specifications. The project team should make every effort to minimize rework.

NOTE: Look at the first sentence. It says "Quality should be designed into, not inspected into." We do not inspect quality into something. You may be asked a few questions that lure you into the idea that going back and inspecting for quality is the right answer. IT IS NOT. We design quality so that it's built in. Remember, responsibility for quality rests with the person who owns that given activity. Quality on the project is the responsibility of the project manager. Quality on a task is the responsibility of the person doing that task.

CHAPTER REVIEW

1. The quality management plan describes all the following with the exception of the:
    A. Method for implementing the quality policy
    B. Project quality system
    C. Organizational structure, responsibilities, procedures, processes, and resources needed to implement project quality management
    D. Procedures used to conduct quality analyses between cost and schedule

2. The quality management processes do not include:
    A. Quality assurance
    B. Quality planning
    C. Overall change control
    D. Quality control

3. _____ identifies which quality standards are relevant to the project and determines how to satisfy them.
    A. Quality assurance
    B. Process control
    C. Quality control
    D. Quality planning

4. _____ monitors specific project results to determine if they comply with relevant quality standards and identifies ways to eliminate causes of unsatisfactory performance.
    A. Quality assurance
    B. Quality planning
    C. Process control
    D. Quality control

5. According to PMI, the statistical control chart is a tool used primarily to help:
    A. Monitor process variation over time
    B. Measure the degree of conformance
    C. Determine whether results conform to project scope
    D. Determine whether results conform to stakeholder requirements

6. As senior project manager you were recently asked to review the manufacturing line at General Motors. While performing your review you found poor quality control, poorly stocked supply bins and outdated machinery. You decide to prepare your results for management using a Pareto diagram to display your findings because it is an excellent way to:
    A. Show how many results were generated, by type or category of identified cause
    B. Forecast future outcomes based on historical lessons
    C. Show which variables have the most influence on the overall project status
    D. Show how various causes tend to create potential problems or effects

7. Which of the following is an internal failure cost?
    A. Training
    B. Rework
    C. In-process testing
    D. Lab testing

8. According to PMI and the PMBOK Guide, which of the following statements best describes attribute sampling versus variable sampling?
    A. Attribute sampling is concerned with unique causes, whereas variable sampling is concerned with multiple causes.
    B. Attribute sampling is concerned with prevention, whereas variable sampling is concerned with inspection.
    C. Variable sampling is preferred when working with cost flow analysis
    D. Attribute sampling is concerned with conformance, whereas variable sampling is concerned with the degree of conformity.

9. Six sigma refers to the aim of setting tolerance limits at six standard deviations from the mean, whereas the normally expected deviation of a process is known as:
    A. Two standard deviations
    B. One standard deviation
    C. Four standard deviations
    D. Three standard deviations

10. A diagram that shows how various elements of a system relate is called a:
    A. CPM
    B. Flowchart
    C. Bar chart
    D. Network diagram

11. An _____ definition describes, in very specific terms, what something is, and how it is measured by the quality control process.
    A. Process control
    B. Operational
    C. Hierarchical system model
    D. Quality policy

12. _____ is a statistical method that helps identify which factors might influence specific variables.
    A. Contemporaneous scheduling
    B. Critical path method
    C. Benchmarking
    D. Design of experiments

13. Which of the following is an input to the quality assurance process?
    A. Quality management plan
    B. Customer satisfaction
    C. Standards and regulations
    D. Product description

14. Having just returned from a company trip to Japan where you studied manufacturing and learned about the Kaizen philosophy of quality, you have now decided to try and implement this philosophy within your organization. You are explaining to your project team that the Even though your project, installing bunk beds in your company's executive offices so that Kaizen approach to continuous improvement will help emphasize?
    A. The importance of customer satisfaction over cost
    B. Slow moving changes in operating practices
    C. Incremental improvement
    D. Incremental improvement at pre-defined time and stages

15. Which of the following is a tool and technique that can be used in the quality assurance process to identify lessons learned that could improve performance of the project?
    A. Benefit/cost analysis
    B. Flow charting
    C. Quality audits
    D. Benchmarking

16. Quality is now your company motto. Your company just obtained certification under ISO 9000 and now wants the Forbes 100 Quality Award. Each project has a quality statement that is consistent with the organization's vision and mission. Both internal/external quality assurance/control is provided on all projects to:
    A. Monitor project results and note whether they comply with quality control standards
    B. Provide confidence that the project will satisfy relevant quality standards
    C. Assure customers/clients of your commitment
    D. Identify ways to eliminate unsatisfactory results

17. Pareto analysis, cause-and-effect diagrams, and flow charts are tools used in quality
    A. Assurance
    B. Control
    C. Verification
    D. Planning

18. Which of the following is part of modern quality management?
    A. Using Zero Defects as a motivation technique
    B. Considering 95 percent of quality costs the responsibility of management
    C. Addressing both the project management and the product
    D. Relying on frequent inspection

19. According to the PMBOK Guide, when a process is considered to be in control, it
    A. May not be changed to provide improvements
    B. Should not be adjusted
    C. Should not be reworked for any reason
    D. Shows differences caused by internal risks

20. Project quality management must address both the _____ of the project, as well as the _____ of the project.
    A. Quality, schedule
    B. Objectives, organization
    C. Management, product
    D. Customer requirements, stakeholders

The Project Management Professional (PMP®) Exam Guide

ANSWERS

1. D
2. C
3. D
4. D
5. A
6. A
7. B
8. D
9. D
10. B
11. B
12. D
13. A
14. C
15. C
16. B
17. B
18. C
19. B
20. C

PROJECT HUMAN RESOURCE MANAGEMENT

8

The Project Human Resource Management section of the PMP exam focuses heavily on organizational structures, roles and responsibilities of the project manager, team building, and conflict resolution.

In contrast to other areas of the PMBOK Guide in which commonly known terms are used, much of the terminology developed for Project Human Resource Management seems peculiar to PMI. In spite of the unfamiliarity of some terminology, most people do find the human resource questions to be difficult.

Project Human Resource Management involves all aspects of people management and personal interaction including leading, coaching, dealing with conflict, and more. Some of the project participants whom you'll get to practice these skills on include stakeholders, team members, and customers. Each requires the use of different communication styles, leadership skills, and team-building skills. A good project manager knows when to enact certain skills and communication styles based on the situation.

The PMP exam is heavily weighted toward team development (that is, behavioral topics). Only a few questions appear on administrative issues, and they should be relatively easy to answer, given familiarity with general corporate—personnel policies governing your everyday work life.

The questions predominantly focus on forms of organization, project manager roles and responsibilities, types of power, project conflict, conflict management, and team building.

FORMS OF ORGANIZATION
PMI recognizes six approaches to project organizational structure, and those are as follows:

FUNCTIONAL
In a functional organizational structure, a project is assigned to the functional department that is best equipped to implement the project or that is most capable of ensuring the project's success.

When using the functional organizational form to complete a project, the tam comprises individuals from the functional department to which the project is assigned. This structure not only allows individuals to use their expertise and demonstrate special abilities, but also presents them opportunities for professional growth.

A downside to this organizational structure is that no single person has full accountability for the project, which increases the likelihood that the project will fail. Since the project manager is not given much formal authority, the functional organizational structure placed the project manager in the weakest position of all the organizational structures.

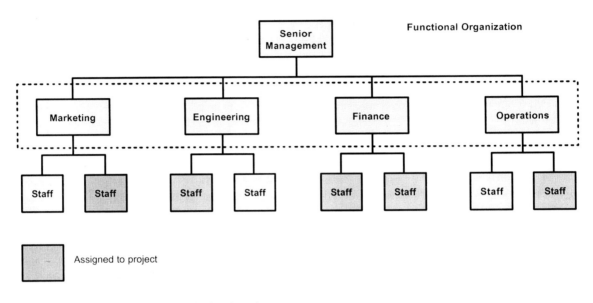

Assigned to project

- - - - - -   Represents project communication channel

PROJECT EXPEDITOR

This form of organization retains the functional specialization but adds a project expeditor who serves as a communication link and coordinator for the project across the various functional units. The expeditor cannot personally make or enforce decisions. This form is used in cases in which a project's cost and importance are relatively low.

PROJECT COORDINATOR

The project coordinator organization is similar to the project expeditor structure, except that the coordinator reports to a higher-level manager than do functional managers. Accordingly, the project coordinator has some authority to assign work to individuals within the functional units.

WEAK MATRIX

A matrix organizational structure is a combination of functional and purely project structures. In a weak matrix organizational structure, the project manager has a low level of authority. The project manager is in charge of making sure activities are completed but cannot do certain things such as reallocate resources or make changes to a project's schedule.

Lack of authority to make project-related decisions puts the project manager at a disadvantage, so in order to ensure that project goals are met, the project manager must use technical and interpersonal skills to influence the direction of the project.

In some instances, the project manager is given some authority, but must share that authority with a functional manager. Shared authority often results in power struggles that disrupt the project environment and can jeopardize the successful completion of a project.

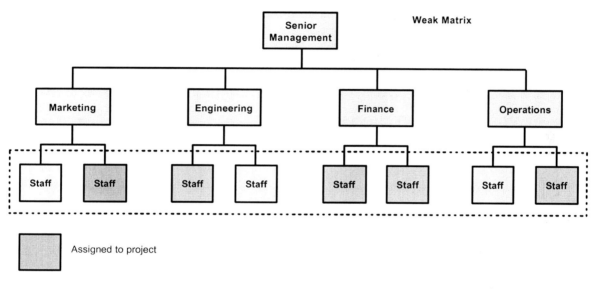

Assigned to project

- - - - - - Represents project communication channel

STRONG MATRIX

A strong matrix organizational structure is similar to a purely project structure in that the project manager has full decision-making authority. However, unlike a purely project organization, a strong matrix does not separate a project from the parent organization.

There is a general division of responsibility in the matrix organizational structure. For example, the project manager controls what the project team does and when they do it, while the functional manager controls who is assigned to the project and what technology is used.

Despite this division of responsibility, a strong matrix does not eliminate role ambiguity between project and functional managers. To avoid conflicts, the project and functional managers must communicate, negotiate, and be flexible when deciding who is responsible for what activities. The project manager has medium to high formal authority.

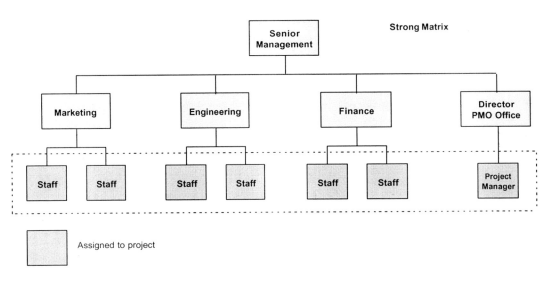

BALANCED MATRIX

The balanced matrix is a structure that includes some weak matrix characteristics and some strong matrix characteristics. In this structure, the project manager's authority is considered to below to moderate given that only 15 to 60 percent of the organization's personnel are assigned to project work.

PROJECTIZED

In a projectized organization, a separate, vertical structure is established for each project. Personnel are assigned to particular projects on a full-time basis. The project manager has total authority over the project, which is subject only to the time, cost, and performance constraints specified in the project targets.

COMPOSITE

The composite organization shows that most modern organizations involve all the organizational structures at various levels. Even an organization that is structured as a classic functional

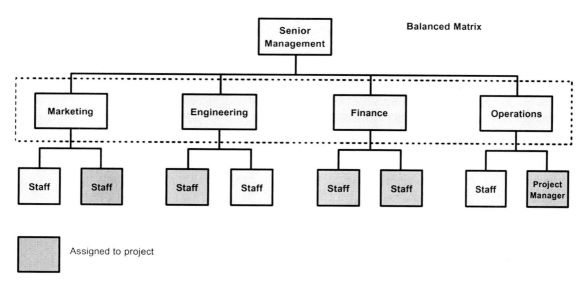

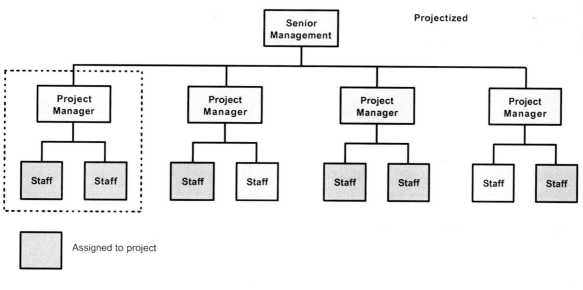

organization may create a special project team to handle a critical project. This team may then have characteristics of a fully projectized structure and may use full-time staff members for the work.

NOTE: All forms of organizations are pretty well described here, but you will want to know that there are functional organizations and project expeditors, which are little more than functionaries and help support the idea of project management, without really practicing itthe practice; the project coordinator is a step up from that. A weak matrix is where the project manager gets resources from functional organizations; a strong matrix is where the balance of power has shifted to the project manager. The way to determine if the balance of power has shifted is to note where the money and the reporting flow from. If all money and reports are generated by the project and are respected as being from the project, then it is a strong matrix. If the functional organizations are seen as generating revenue for the organization rather than the project organizations, then it is a weak matrix. And if it is a mix? It is a balanced matrix

PMI's ideal organization is one that is projectized; it's a place where the project has its own little home within the organization. You should know that a project manager is a professional in the eyes of PMI.

PROJECT INTERFACES

PMI discusses three types of interfaces that should be considered in organizational planning. You should be familiar with each one and with specific examples. These interfaces often occur simultaneously.

- Organizational interfaces - deal with the types of reporting relationships that exist within an organization's structure, be they functional, matrix, or projectized..
- Technical interfaces - deal with the reporting relationships that exist within the technical areas of an organization.
- Interpersonal interfaces - deal with the relationships that exist among project team members and among other project participants.

ORGANIZATIONAL PLANNING CONSTRAINTS

Constraints are discussed in almost all of the project management knowledge areas. In human resource management, a number of constraints are mentioned. Organizational planning, in particular, is affected by constraints such as the following:

- The organizational structure of the performing organization: Organizational structures can become a constraint. For example, a strong matrix structure provides the project manager with much more authority and power than the weak matrix structure.
- Collective bargaining agreements: Collective bargaining agreements with unions and contractual obligations with other organized employee associations may require specialized reporting relationships and are considered constraints.

- Team Preferences: Partiality of the project management team might be a constraint. Failure or success with a certain organizational structure in the past might lead team members to prefer one type of team or organizational structure over another type.
- Expected staff assignments: The organization of the project team should be influenced by the skills, experience and knowledge of the project team members who wills operate on the team. This constraint is called expected staff assignments.

KEY ORGANIZATIONAL PLANNING OUTPUT

- **Role and responsibility assignments -** Project roles in this context refer to the project manager, project team member, and stakeholders. The roles and responsibilities for this process are tied to the project scope and the work breakdown structure. Many times a project manager will design and use Responsibility Assignment Matrix (See PMBOK Guide figure 9.2) to graphically display this information. Note the importance of linking these roles and responsibilities to scope definition, and know the purpose of and how to prepare a responsibility assignment matrix.
- **Staffing management plan -** This plan documents how and when people resources will be introduced to the project and then upon completion of the project how they will be released. Recognize that project managers may have responsibilities for human resource redeployment and release. Resource histograms often are part of this plan (see PMBOK Guide figure 9.3).
- **Organization chart -** This type of chart shows the reporting relationship of the project team members. Note that the organizational breakdown structure, discussed also in the scope definition section, is a type of organization chart that shows which organizational units are responsible for which work packages.

STAFF ACQUISITION

The staff acquisition process involves obtaining and assigning personnel to perform project activities. The project manager's goal during staff acquisition is to obtain personnel who have the skills that are outlined in the project's staff management plan.

It is important to understand that acquiring staff is a component of the human resource management variable and is also part of the planning step of the project management process. A key input to this process is the staffing pool description. Before acquiring staff for a project, it is helpful to answer the following questions:

- What type of organizational structure will be used for the project?
- Who should be on the project team?
- What skills would each team member bring to the project?
- Will team members work well together?
- What can result when the project loses a key team member?

Because staff assignments must be negotiated on most projects, negotiating is a principal tool and technique. Negotiation is defined as the art of achieving what you want from a transaction, leaving all other parties involved content that the relationship has gone well. Negotiating for project personnel is not an easy task. The most critical element of successful negotiating is preparation. **NEVER GO INTO A NEGOTIATION PROCESS UNLESS YOU ARE PREPARED.**

Negotiating also relates to the project manager's ability to influence the organization to "get things done," so again, review the definitions for power and politics. PMI explains that the team's influencing competencies and politics play an important role in negotiating staff assignments. For example, a functional manager may be rewarded based on staff utilization. This in turn creates an incentive for this manager to assign available staff who may not meet all the project's requirements.

PROJECT MANAGER ROLES AND RESPONSIBILITIES

PMI defines the functions, roles, qualifications, and education and experience requirements of the project manager as follows:

FUNCTIONS OF THE PROJECT MANAGER

- Planning, scheduling, and estimating
- Performance, cost, and trend analysis
- Progress reporting
- Maintaining client/consultant relations
- Logistics management
- Cost control
- Procedure writing and administration
- Interface management (identifying; documenting; scheduling; communicating; and monitoring personnel, organizational, and system interfaces relating to the project)
- Integration of the efforts of project subsystems
- PMI considers planning, organizing, leading, and controlling the four most important functions of the project manager. Effective management of the dual reporting relationship— a situation in which team members are accountable to both a project manager and a functional manager—generally is the project manager's responsibility.

ROLES OF THE PROJECT MANAGER

- Integrator
- Communicator
- Team leader
- Decision maker
- Climate creator/builder

QUALIFICATIONS OF THE PROJECT MANAGER

- Works well with others
- Experienced in his or her area of expertise
- Supervisory experience
- Familiar with contract administration
- Able to accurately present the company's position
- Profit-oriented
- A qualified negotiator
- Experience and Education Requirements of the Project Manager
- Formal college education desirable
- Continuing education in topics such as negotiation, conflict management, group dynamics, and leadership
- Experience as a functional manager, or preferably, a project management assistant

TYPES OF POWER

According to PMI, the project manager can exert the following types of power:

LEGITIMATE POWER

Legitimate power is derived from the person's formal position within the organization. The project manager's ability to use this power derives from his or her position in the organizational hierarchy and his or her degree of control over the project, as modified by the organizational climate. Use of this power should be in conjunction with expert and reward power whenever possible.

COERCIVE POWER

Coercive power is predicated on fear (for example, a subordinate fears being deprived of something for failing to do what the supervisor asks). The ability to use this power derives from the project manager's control over the project and project personnel.

REWARD POWER

Reward power involves positive reinforcement and the ability to award people something of value in exchange for their cooperation. The project manager's ability to use this power derives from his or her position in the organizational hierarchy and degree of control over the project.

EXPERT POWER

Expert power can only be exercised by individuals who are held in particular esteem because of their special knowledge or skill. The project manager's ability to use this power derives from reputation, knowledge, and experience.

REFERENT POWER

Referent power is based on citing the authority of a more powerful person (for example, one's supervisor or someone's spouse is the CEO) as the basis for one's own authority. The project manager's ability to use this power derives from his or her position in the organizational hierarchy.

NOTE: PMI recommends that project managers rely on reward and expert power to the greatest extent possible, and that they avoid use of coercive power. Please be aware that in addition to the above list, other project management luminaries have also coined terms to describe forms of power or influence. These terms include:

- **Purse-string power** - Denotes budget or spending authority held by the project manager
- **Bureaucratic power** - The ability of the project manager to use the rules and procedures of the organization to maximize personal effectiveness.
- **Charismatic power** - Power and influence derived from the project manager's personality and persona to encourage people to accomplish things they may not be inclined to do.
- **Penalty power** - Involves negative reinforcement and the ability to withhold something of value as a response to lack of cooperation or poor performance.

NOTE: What types of power do we have as a project manager? Legitimate, coercive, reward, expert and referent. The thing that is critical here is to recognize that reward and expert power are the best kinds of power that a project manager can exert. The worst kind, from PMI's perspective, is coercive power—power by virtue of threat.

PROJECT CONFLICT

PMI considers dealing with conflict to be absolutely necessary to improving team behaviors.

WHY CONFLICT IS UNAVOIDABLE ON PROJECTS

- High-stress environment
- Ambiguous roles
- Multiple bosses
- Prevalence of advanced technology concerns

SEVEN SOURCES OF CONFLICT IN PROJECT ENVIRONMENTS

- Project priorities
- Administrative procedures
- Technical opinions and performance trade-offs
- Personnel resources
- Cost
- Schedules
- Personalities

NOTE: Among these sources, PMI considers conflict over program priorities, personnel resources, technical issues, and scheduling problems to create the most tension in the project management environment.

Every project has conflicts and PMI wants you to understand that. It also want you to know why that happens and the sources for conflict. Make sure you know that PMI considers conflict over program priorities, personnel resources, technical issues, and scheduling problems as being the ones that cause the most tension in the project environment.

CONFLICT AND THE PROJECT LIFE CYCLE

The highest-ranked sources of conflict evident in each phase of the life cycle are

- Concept phase - Project priorities, administrative procedures, and schedules
- Development phase - Project priorities, schedules, and administrative procedures
- Implementation phase - Schedules, technical issues, and personnel resources
- Termination phase - Schedules, personality conflicts, and personnel resources

CONFLICT MANAGEMENT

Whether conflict has a net positive or negative effect on a project and its parent organization depends on how the project manager handles it. PMI recognizes these five methods for dealing with conflict:

PROBLEM SOLVING (OR CONFRONTATION)

With problem solving, the project manager addresses conflict directly in a problem-solving mode to get the parties working together to define the problem, collect information, develop and analyze alternatives, and select the most appropriate alternative.

NOTE: PMI recommends problem solving as the conflict resolution method of choice.

COMPROMISING

Compromising consists of bargaining and searching for solutions that attempt to bring some degree of satisfaction to the conflicting parties. Neither party wins but each may get some degree of satisfaction.

NOTE. PMI considers this the second-best conflict resolution mode, after problem solving/confrontation.

SMOOTHING

Smoothing consists of de-emphasizing the opponents' differences and emphasizing their commonalties over the issues in question. Smoothing keeps the atmosphere friendly, but avoids solving the root causes of the conflict.

WITHDRAWAL

Withdrawal is defined as retreating from actual or potential disagreements and conflict situations. It is really a delaying tactic that fails to resolve the conflict but does cool down the situation temporarily.

FORCING

Forcing consists of exerting one's viewpoint at the potential expense of another party, thus establishing a win-lose situation.

NOTE: PMI recommends using forcing only as a last resort, because it can cause additional conflicts as antagonism builds.

As you look at the various ways that we can manage conflict, PMI's preferred approach is the very first one: problem solving/confrontation. PMI will almost always in the PMP exam recognize this as confrontation rather than problem solving. That makes it a little harder to recognize the most positive or the most optimistic way to approach a particular problem. Confrontation is always the PMI approach.

TEAM BUILDING

Team building is a key tool and technique for team development. PMI points out the difficulty of developing a team in a matrix organization structure in which team members must report to a project manager and a functional manager and in which development as a team is critical to the project's ability to meet its objectives. Team development serves to promote performance improvements both in terms of individual skills and in team behaviors. A mandatory prerequisite for team building is commitment from top management.

PMI recommends a concerted team-building effort at the start of every new project.

GOALS AND RESULTS OF PROJECT TEAM BUILDING
- Team members are interdependent
- There is a consensus on well-defined project goals and objectives
- Team members are committed to working together
- Team is accountable as a functioning unit within the larger organization
- There is a moderate level of competition and conflict

SYMPTOMS OF POOR TEAMWORK
- Frustration
- Conflict and unhealthy competition
- Unproductive meetings
- Lack of trust or confidence in the project manager

GROUND RULES FOR PROJECT TEAM BUILDING

- Start as soon as possible
- Continue team building throughout the life of the project
- Recruit the best possible people
- Make sure that everyone who will significantly contribute to the project, full- or part-time, is on the team
- Obtain team agreement on all major actions
- Recognize the existence of team politics but stay out of them
- Behave as a role model
- Use delegation as the best way to assure commitment
- Don't try to force or manipulate team members
- Regularly evaluate team effectiveness
- Plan and use a team-building process

THE TEAM-BUILDING PROCESS

PLAN FOR TEAM BUILDING

- Carefully define project roles and assignments
- Ensure project goals and members' personal goals coincide

NEGOTIATE FOR TEAM MEMBERS

- Obtain the most promising personnel available
- Choose candidates with both technical expertise and potential to be effective team members

ORGANIZE THE TEAM

- Make specific assignments to specific people
- Prepare and circulate responsibility matrixes

HOLD A KICKOFF MEETING

- Set technical and procedural agendas
- Ensure sufficient time for members to get to know one another
- Establish working relationships and communications

OBTAIN TEAM MEMBER COMMITMENTS

- Time commitment
- Role commitment
- Project priority commitment
- Build communication links

CONDUCT TEAM-BUILDING EXERCISES

INCORPORATE TEAM-BUILDING ACTIVITIES INTO ALL PROJECT ACTIVITIES

- Meetings, planning sessions, and technical/schedule reviews
- Group and individual counseling sessions
- Recognition of outstanding performance

NOTE: A project manager needs to realize that establishing trust should be the first step in generating positive team performance, when project team members are not collocated.

Look down this list of issues associated with team building. What you want to remember are the things that make team building sound great, make it sound positive, and make it sound like something every project should strive for on a regular basis.

CHARACTERISTICS OF EFFECTIVE GROUPS

- Clearly defined goals
- Open, goal-directed communication
- Equally shared power
- Flexible decision making
- Controversy considered healthy
- Diversity encouraged
- Evident interpersonal problem-solving

CHARACTERISTICS OF INEFFECTIVE GROUPS

- Goals vague or imposed without discussion
- Communication guarded
- Power with leader—not shared
- Decision making without consultation
- Controversy and conflict not tolerated
- Individual resources not utilized
- Undervalue of member contributions

PROBLEMS WITH GROUPS

- Splitting: clique and/or opposing groups
- Hidden Agendas: past baggage gets in the way of group goals and work
- Social Loafing: slacking off to let (force) other members complete majority of work
- Destructive Behavior: damaging to group and individuals; must be dealt with by leader

ROLE FUNCTIONS OF MEMBERS

- Maintenance: make others feel good
- Aggressor: attacks other members
- Blocker: rejects and argues to block the work of the others
- Joker: does not take work seriously
- Avoider: whispers, doodles, passive
- Self confessor: works on personal issues
- Recognition seeker: seeks to be the center of attention

COLLOCATION

Collocation is an approach in which all team members are brought together in one location. It has proven to be beneficial for team development. PMI states that collocation is effective in facilitating better communications and rapid team building. PMI also notes that collocation may be impractical at times but should be considered when drastic steps are indicated because it effectively prevents dilution of the project effort by decreasing distractions and focusing the entire team on the same problems.

MOTIVATION THEORIES

Four theories are of particular importance: Maslow's hierarchy of needs, McGregor's Theory X and Theory Y, Herzberg's Theory of Motivation, and the Expectancy Theory.

MASLOW'S HIERARCHY OF NEEDS

According to Maslow's Hierarchy of Needs, people have the following five kinds of needs:

- Physiological needs, of which the most important are the need for food and other things necessary for survival
- The need for safety—from danger, threat, and deprivation
- Social needs for association with one's fellows, for friendship, and love
- The need for self-respect, self-esteem, the respect of one's fellows, status
- The need for self-fulfillment through the development of powers and skills, and a chance to use creativity (self-actualization)

Maslow theorized that people are driven to satisfy survival needs first, followed by safety needs, and so on. Once these needs are fulfilled, the drive to fulfill them goes away until the needs arise again. The application to human resource management is that certain needs must be met in order for people to function at their peak physical and mental levels, enabling them to fulfill their project responsibilities.

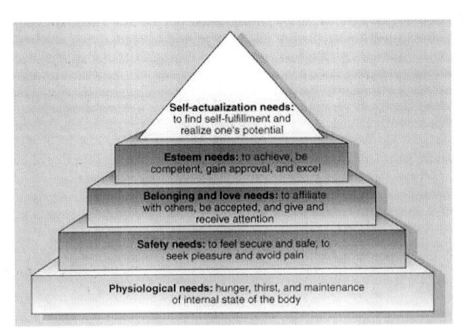

Maslow's Hierarchy of Needs

DOUGLAS MCGREGOR

According to Douglas McGregor's Theory X, the average person is lazy, avoiding work and responsibility whenever possible, needs constant supervision, and is motivated to work only when threatened. McGregor's Theory Y suggests that the average person is willing to work without constant supervision.

A project manager who agrees with Theory X is strict with team members, motivating them with undesirable consequences. This kind of project manager does not allow team members to participate in making project decisions.

A project manager who agrees with Theory Y motivates team members by allowing them to work with little supervision and encourages participation in making project decisions. Allowing team members to work somewhat independently can build confidence. Listening to their input before making decisions can strengthen team members' commitment to a project.

THEORY X

With Theory X assumptions, management's role is to coerce and control employees.

- People have an inherent dislike for work and will avoid it whenever possible.
- People must be coerced, controlled, directed, or threatened with punishment in order to get them to achieve the organizational objectives.
- People prefer to be directed, do not want responsibility, and have little or no ambition.
- People seek security above all else.

THEORY Y

With Theory Y assumptions, management's role is to develop the potential in employees and help them to release that potential toward common goals.

- Work is as natural as play and rest.
- People will exercise self-direction if they are committed to the objectives (they are not lazy).
- Commitment to objectives is a function of the rewards associated with their achievement.
- People learn to accept and seek responsibility.
- Creativity, ingenuity, and imagination are widely distributed among the population. People are capable of using these abilities to solve an organizational problem.
- People have potential.

THEORY Z

Theory Z was developed by William Ouchi, in his 1982 book *Theory Z: How American management can Meet the Japanese Challenge*.

Theory Z is often referred to as the '"Japanese" management style, which is essentially what it is. Theory Z essentially advocates a combination of all that's best about theory Y and modern Japanese management, which places a large amount of freedom and trust with workers, and assumes that workers have a strong loyalty and interest in team-working and the organization. Theory Z also places more reliance on the attitude and responsibilities of the workers, whereas McGregor's XY theory is mainly focused on management and motivation from the manager's and organization's perspective.

HERZBERG'S THEORY OF MOTIVATION

Frederick Herzberg constructed a two-dimensional paradigm of factors affecting people's attitudes about work. He concluded that such factors as company policy, supervision, interpersonal relations, working conditions, and salary are hygiene factors rather than motivators. According to the theory, the absence of hygiene factors can create job dissatisfaction, but their presence does not motivate or create satisfaction.

In contrast, he determined from the data that the motivators were elements that enriched a person's job; he found five factors in particular that were strong determiners of job satisfaction: achievement, recognition, the work itself, responsibility, and advancement. These motivators (satisfiers) were associated with long-term positive effects in job performance while the hygiene factors (dissatisfiers) consistently produced only short-term changes in job attitudes and performance, which quickly fell back to its previous level.

In summary, satisfiers describe a person's relationship with what she or he does, many related to the tasks being performed. Dissatisfiers, on the other hand, have to do with a person's relationship to the context or environment in which she or he performs the job. The satisfiers relate to what a person does while the dissatisfiers relate to the situation in which the person does what he or she does.

EXPECTANCY THEORY

Expectancy theory holds that people will tend to be highly productive and motivated if the following two conditions are satisfied: (1) people believe that their efforts will likely lead to successful results and (2) those people also believe they will be rewarded for their success.

NOTE: Expectancy theory says two things. One, you get what you expect—self-fulfilling prophecy. The other is, if people think that their outcomes are going to be significant, if they think they are going to matter in terms of the organization, then they do better. People like to be involved in something where they think they are making a difference.

REWARD AND RECOGNITION SYSTEMS

PMI explains that people are motivated in direct proportion to the value they feel is being placed on them. Rewards demonstrate this value. Reward and recognition systems are formal ways of recognizing and promoting desirable behavior. To be effective, the link between project performance and reward must be clear, explicit, and achievable. In addition to rewarding individuals for outstanding work, team incentive rewards are effective motivators. If the organization does not have a reward system, or if that reward system is inappropriate for project-based work, then the project should have its own reward and recognition system. It is desirable for project staff to provide input to the appraisals of any project staff members with whom they interact in a significant way. PMI suggests that a good rule for project managers is to give the team all the glory possible during the life cycle of the project because there may be little left at the end.

PERSONNEL ISSUES

The project manager or project teams rarely have the responsibility of the administration of the human resource procedures. These matters are typically handled by the personnel department.However, you should be aware of any administrative requirements to ensure compliance. A variety of personnel issues may appear on the exam, such as the following:

- Fringe benefits: Education, training, profit sharing, medical benefits, and the employer's matching of 401(k) contributions, and so on.

- Perquisites or "perks": A window office, a corner office, use of the executive dining room, special parking space, a company car, and so on.
- Arbitration: A technique for resolving conflict in which the parties agree to have a neutral third party hear the dispute and make a decision. The parties agree in advance to abide by this decision.
- Productivity: Measured as a ratio that divides some measure of output by the input required. For example, the number of items produced per hour of labor.
- Human resource functions: Aside from the traditional role of hiring, there are several other important functions often performed by human resource departments. These include training, career planning, and team building.

NOTE: One big thing to remember out of this is knowing the difference between a fringe and a perk. A fringe benefit is something provided across the organization to anyone who is eligible for it. A perk is something given to an individual based on individual performance.

CHAPTER REVIEW

1. Which theory is based on the assumption that people need to be watched every minute, that they are incapable and avoid responsibility?
    A. Theory Y
    B. Herzberg's theory
    C. Theory Z
    D. Theory X

2. You are the project manager for a new systems project dealing with aircraft cargo holds. Management of course wants your project to yield a high-value but at a low cost. You have been reading several documents and realize that you would like to take the time and money to incorporate features that would increase long-term project value, but one of your major vendors employs senior-level staff who typically cost more than other vendors. When working with stakeholders, you should:
    A. Be sensitive to the fact that stakeholders often have very different objectives and that this makes stakeholder management difficult
    B. Group stakeholders into categories for easy identification
    C. Try to manage and control stakeholders
    D. Recognize that roles and responsibilities may overlap

3. You and your project team have started working on a complex project that you have been told is a make or brake opportunity for your business. Most of the application can be built in house but there is one component that will need to be outsourced. No one on the project team has any contract administration experience, and no contracts department staff can be assigned to the project. To ensure that you create a successful relationship with the prospective seller, you must provide two team members with project procurement management training. Direct and indirect training costs should be:
    A. Paid for by your organization
    B. Charged to the project budget
    C. Paid for by the subcontractor
    D. Considered an input to cost budgeting

4. The primary outputs of team development are:
    A. Improved project performance and high team morale
    B. Staffing management and high team morale
    C. High team morale and inputs to performance appraisals
    D. Improved project performance and inputs to performance appraisals

5. According to Douglas McGregor, Theory X management is based on the assumption that:
    A. Quality improvements lie in the hands of quality circles
    B. Profits are tied to meeting the project' baseline milestones
    C. Absenteeism is tied to poor working conditions
    D. Workers are inherently unmotivated and need strong guidance

6. Your project has been under way for some time, but indicators show that it is in trouble. You have observed all the following symptoms of bad teamwork in your project team except:
    A. Frustration
    B. Unproductive meetings
    C. Lack of trust or confidence in the project manager
    D. Excessive meetings

7. The major difference between the project coordinator and project expeditor forms of organization is that:
    A. The project coordinator reports to a higher-level manager in the organization
    B. The project expeditor acts only as a liaison between senior management and the project team
    C. The project coordinator cannot personally make decisions
    D. Strong commitment to the project usually does not exist in the project expeditor form of organization

8. One way for a project manager to promote positive team performance in project teams, whose members are not collocated is to do which of the following:
    A. Build trust
    B. Develop a reward/recognition system
    C. Obtain the support of the functional managers in the other locations
    D. Send out weekly WBS updates

9. Which of the following represents a constraint on the staff acquisition process:
    A. Pre-assignment of staff to the project
    B. Recruitment practices of the organizations involved
    C. Team member training requirements
    D. Use of outsourcing to free up resources

10. You have just been hired as a project coordinator, what type of environment are you now working in?
    A. Strong matrix
    B. Projectized
    C. Balanced matrix
    D. Weak matrix

11. According to PMI what is the worst type of power that a project manage can use?
    A. Formal
    B. Penalty
    C. Referent
    D. Reward

12. A constraining factor that may possibly affect the organization of the project team is:
    A. Poor communication among team members
    B. Functional type management
    C. Ambiguous staffing requirements
    D. The organizational structure of the performing organization

13. Inputs to Team Development include all of the following except:
    A. Project staff
    B. Reward and recognition systems
    C. Performance reports
    D. Project plan

14. Performance improvements include all of the following except:
    A. Improvements in amount of overtime worked
    B. Improvements in individual skills
    C. Improvements in team behaviors
    D. Improvements in team capabilities

15. A graphic display of resource usage hours is known as:
    A. Organizational chart
    B. Responsibility matrix
    C. WBS
    D. Histogram

16. Which is not among the tools and techniques of Organizational Planning:
    A. Staffing management plan
    B. Templates
    C. Human resource practices
    D. Organizational theory

17. During the team meeting, today you noticed that one team member was criticizing of the others. This person was assuming which of the following destructive team roles:
    A. Aggressor
    B. Blocker
    C. Recognition seeker
    D. Dominator

18. As a project manager, you realize that an important part of the staffing plan is releasing personnel when they are no longer needed on a project. All of the following are benefits of properly addressing this issue except:
    A. Reduces costs
    B. Improves morale
    C. Aids in staffing future projects
    D. Defines proper chain of command

19. According to PMI, a project manager must have all of the following skills and know when and how to use them on a project except:
    A. Directing
    B. Supportive
    C. Facilitating
    D. Collaborating

20. According to Maslow's Hierarchy of Needs, a person who is attempting to fulfill the need for safety has already satisfied which needs?
    A. Esteem
    B. Self-Actualization
    C. Physiological
    D. Social

ANSWERS

1. D
2. A
3. A
4. D
5. D
6. D
7. A
8. A
9. B
10. D
11. B
12. D
13. B
14. A
15. D
16. A
17. A
18. D
19. D
20. C

PROJECT COMMUNICATIONS MANAGEMENT

The Project Communications Management questions on the PMP exam are basic and are taken primarily from the PMBOK Guide and other PMI published materials. Common sense and your own expertise will play a large role in your ability to answer the questions on this topic.

PMI considers management style to be an essential component of how a project manager communicates, and thinks of the kickoff meeting as one of the most effective mechanisms in Project Communications Management. The questions on the exam about this focus on formal and informal communication, verbal versus written communication, conflict resolution, and management styles.

The processes that make up the Project Communications Management knowledge area are as follows: Communications Planning, Information Distribution, Performance Reporting, and Administrative Closure.

The processes in the Project Communications knowledge area are related to general communication skills but aren't the same thing. Communication skills are considered general management skills that the project manager utilizes on a daily basis. The processes in the Communications knowledge area seek to ensure that all project information including project plans, risk assessments, meeting notes, and more is collected and documented. These processes also ensure information is distributed and shared with appropriate stakeholders and project members. At project closure, the information is archived and used as a reference for future projects. This is referred to as historical information in several project processes.

THE COMMUNICATIONS MODEL

According to PMI, the communications model consists of four major parts, as indicated below:

- <u>Sender:</u> The originator of the message.
- <u>Message:</u> Thoughts, feelings, or ideas, reduced to "code" that are understandable by both sender and receiver.
- <u>Medium:</u> The vehicle or method used to convey the message. The choice of medium will color and influence the effect of the message. The most common media are visual, audio, and tactile.
- <u>Receiver:</u> The person for whom the message is intended. He or she must accept and understand the message before communication has taken place.

The receiver may filter the information, that is, selectively reduce its quantity or quality. If the receiver is actively listening, he or she is attentive and asks for clarification or repetition of ambiguous messages. The sender should request feedback to ensure the message has been received in its entirety.

COMMUNICATION CHANNELS

As the scope of a project grows, it is also natural in most cases for the size of the project team to grow. In fact, it is known that the number of possible communication channels among project team members is determined by the following formula: $(n^2 - n) \div 2$ where "n" represents the number of people on the team. Know this formula!

Using the formula above—$(n^2 - n) \div 2$—we could calculate the communication channel for the picture above. Based on the formula and information given $(5^2 - 5) \div 2 = (25 - 5) \div 2 = 20 \div 2 = 10$ different communication channels.

NOTE: A sample exam question may be similar to this: If you have a communication team with five members and you add four more people to the team, how many additional communication channels were added?

Such a mathematical relationship is known as a geometric series. In ordinary language this simply means that as team size grows, the number of potential communication channels grows at greater than a linear rate. Although not everyone on the team needs to communicate with everyone else on each type of communication, the potential exists to overwhelm the team with communication requirements. Accordingly, the larger a team grows the more important it is for the project manager to reorganize the team structure to enhance formal communications.

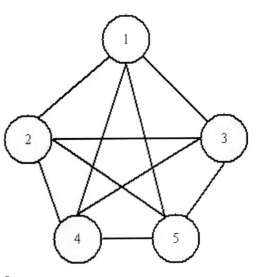

NOTE: There is an easy way to handle this on the exam if you do not want to memorize the mathematical formula. When it comes to communications channels, think of it as a game of connecting the dots. All you need to do is draw a circle to represent each participant in the communications loop. Let's say there are four members in the communications loop. You draw the line from the first circle over to the other three, then from the second to the remaining two, and from the third to the remaining one. What you wind up with is a series of lines connecting them. That series of lines represents the number of communications channels that must exist, and is the same as the formula $(n^2 - n) \div 2$.

COMMUNICATIONS PLANNING

The project communications variable is broken down into the following components: communications planning, distributing information, performance reporting, and concluding a project. Project communication is a project variable that consists of orchestrating timely, accurate, and concise distribution of project data and updates to the appropriate people. The goal of project communication is to make sure everyone involved in a project has the information they need to fulfill their responsibilities.

A project's success or failure depends largely on the quality of communication within the project team, within the project's parent organization, and outside the project, with contractors and vendors. The smallest breakdown in communication can result in project failure. Therefore, project communication should be a priority during project planning and throughout project execution.

COMMUNICATIONS REQUIREMENTS

Once you have identified a project's stakeholders, the next step is to determine what their information requirements are. When determining information requirements, it is helpful to answer the following questions:

- Who is responsible for which project activities?
- Where are the stakeholders located?
- When do stakeholders want information?
- How often do stakeholders want information?
- What kinds of information do stakeholders want?

COMMUNICATIONS TECHNOLOGY

Once you have determined what information the project's stakeholders need, you must decide how to get them the necessary information. The means of communication depends on such things as proximity of stakeholders, their level of involvement in a project, and the type of information they both need and want.

For example, if project team members work in close proximity to each other, then hardcopy reports, e-mail messages, meetings and telephone calls are appropriate. If stakeholders want to see progress reports but are thousands of miles from the project site, then reports can be faxed or e-mailed to them.

STAKEHOLDER ANALYSIS

Conducting a stakeholder analysis enables you to identify all project stakeholders. It should consider methods and technologies suited to the project that will provide the information needed to ensure that resources are not wasted on unnecessary information or inappropriate technology. You must also consider information distribution when considering or defining stakeholders.

COMMUNICATIONS MANAGEMENT PLAN

The communications management plan is the output of the communications planning process and is a subsidiary component of the project plan. It should provide the following information:

- Specific guidelines for information collection and storage
- A distribution outline directing how and to whom information should be given
- Clear descriptions of the information that should be distributed, including the level of detail, layout, subject matter, technical definitions, and naming conventions.
- A schedule that designates when information must be collected and distributed.
- Instructions on how to get information between the scheduled distribution times.
- Directives for altering the communications management plan.

INFORMATION DISTRIBUTION

Information distribution is vital to a project's success. People need information to fulfill their responsibilities to a project. If project team members do not have access to the information they need, then they cannot complete their activities effectively.

In addition, distributing information allows stakeholders to see what progress has been made on a project, as well as what changes have been, or should be, made.

It is important to understand that distributing information is not only a component of the communications variable, but also part of the third step of the project management process—executing.

There are a number of ways information is distributed during project execution. The following are some common means of information distribution:

- Written, which includes reports, memos, spreadsheets, business letters, faxes, and files.
- Oral, which includes presentations, meetings, and conference calls.
- Multimedia, which includes videoconferencing.
- Internet or Intranet, which includes e-mail, Web sites, and online bulletin boards.

The form of communication you use depends on three factors:

- Who is the recipient?
- What is the information?
- When does the recipient need the information?

Suppose a client who lives far away, or who travels frequently wants an update on the project's status every Friday by noon. If the client has regular access to a computer, then the best way to communicate is through e-mail.

The information distribution process results in three outputs: project records, project reports, and project presentations.

FIVE VERBAL COMMUNICATION SKILLS
- Speaking (encoding)
- Writing (encoding)
- Listening (decoding)
- Reading (decoding)
- Thought/Reasoning (encoding and decoding)

KICKOFF MEETING

PMI believes in the value of kickoff meetings, and you may see questions on this topic. In particular, be familiar with the objectives of a kickoff meeting. The following are objectives of a kickoff meeting

- Get team members to know one another
- Establish working relationships and lines of communication
- Set team goals and objectives
- Review project status
- Review project plans
- Identify problem areas
- Establish individual and group responsibilities and accountabilities
- Obtain individual and group commitments

NOTE: Kickoff meetings, from PMI's perspective, are vital. They are a critical component, as team building is a critical component of the kickoff meeting.

BARRIERS TO COMMUNICATION

PMI recognizes the following barriers to effective project communications:

- Lack of clear communications channels
- Physical or temporal distance between the communicator and receiver
- Difficulties with technical language
- Distracting environmental factors (noise)
- Detrimental attitudes (hostility, disbelief)

NOTE: The presence of communication barriers may lead to increased conflict! When it comes to communication barriers, make sure you know these five bullets listed above. Also note that noise is not just loud rumbling noises in the background, but that it can be visual or tactile. Make sure you are aware of the issues of distance, the issues of hostile attitudes, and particularly, when it comes to hostile attitudes, remember the term "communication blocker." That is what hostile attitudes lead to.

COMMUNICATIONS ROLE OF THE PROJECT MANAGER

According to PMI, project managers spend about 90 percent of their time acquiring and communicating information. This includes about two hours a day in meetings and more than an hour a day in one-on-one coaching or interviewing sessions.

The project manager is the key to all project communications and must be skilled at communicating with the following:

- Top management
- The project team
- Competing project teams (peers)
- The customer

NOTE: Notice the first sentence here. It has a statistic in it: 90 percent of our time is spent acquiring and communicating information. That statistic is important because you may run into a question on the exam that asks, what percentage of the project manager's time is spent acquiring and communicating information – 90 percent, 80 percent, 75 percent, 70 percent. Notice I didn't give you any wild low numbers. The number cluster will be kept together. You need to know that it is about 90 percent. Also, remember that communications go laterally, vertically, and diagonally through the organization.

THE PROJECT MANAGER AND THE CUSTOMER

- The project manager must keep both top management and the customer informed of project, technical, budget, and schedule status.
- He or she must also act as top management's representative to the customer and maintain open and friendly relations with the customer.
- The project manager serves as the focal point for ensuring real, two-way communication between the project team and the customer.

BUILDING EFFECTIVE TEAM COMMUNICATION

PMI advises that project managers undertake six actions to ensure effective project team communications:

1. BE AN EFFECTIVE COMMUNICATOR

The project manager must recognize the importance of an interpersonal communications network among team members and encourage their informal communications. Project managers must also recognize that communication is a two-way street; they cannot simply issue orders, but instead must encourage feedback and consensus-building.

2. BE A COMMUNICATION EXPEDITOR

The project manager must bring people together; initiate relationships, which become communications links; and establish both formal (reporting and responsibility) and informal communications channels.

3. AVOID COMMUNICATION BLOCKERS

Communication blockers are negative responses that kill or inhibit innovative ideas. For example:

- "We can't make it work."
- "Don't waste your time, the boss won't like it."
- "Let's be honest, we can't do it."

4. USE A "TIGHT MATRIX"

The project manager should allocate all team members a single office space, rather than allowing them to work on the project from the offices of their functional departments. This prevents dilution of project effort, decreases outside distractions, and focuses the efforts of the entire team on the same problems. The term "tight matrix" is not to be confused with the terms "strong" matrix or "weak" matrix.

5. HAVE A PROJECT "WAR ROOM"

The project manager should establish a single location where the project team or any portion of the project team can get together for any purpose. This room should be for the exclusive use of one project and should provide a repository for project artifacts, records, and up-to-date schedules and status reports. A war room is also called a "control room" or "project information room."

6. CONDUCT EFFECTIVE MEETINGS

Meetings are essential for building teams, making group decisions, solving group problems, and achieving a group consensus. The project manager should adhere to the following guidelines for leading effective meetings that hold the attention and interest of all team members and stakeholders:

- Start on time
- Establish a meeting policy
- Only call a meeting when there is a real need
- Make the purpose of the meeting very clear
- Encourage participation
- Include a team-building element
- Issue minutes
- Follow-up on all task assignments and action items

In a PMI survey of project managers, the respondents said they attended more than six meetings each week. In those meetings, an average of 25 percent of the time was spent on nonproductive items. The three most prevalent responses on why meetings are not effective were:

• Meeting was not properly planned
• Inept leadership
• Undisciplined participants

NOTE: You need to know the difference between a tight matrix in contrast to the strong and weak matrix mentioned in the other sections of the exam. Specifically a tight matrix refers to physical proximity. Keeping team members close together. To that end, to keep a tight matrix you may want to use a project war room where everyone works together.

MANAGEMENT STYLES

The Project Communications Management section of the exam may address the following management styles:

• Authoritarian: Lets individuals know what is expected of them; gives specific guidance; expects adherence to rules and standards.
• Disruptive: Tends to disrupt unity and cause disorder.
• Ethical: Honest and sincere; presses for fair solutions; goes "by the book".
• Combative: Eager to fight or be disagreeable over any situation.
• Conciliatory: Friendly and agreeable; attempts to unite players into a compatible working team.
• Facilitating: Does not interfere with day-to-day task, but is available for help and guidance when needed.
• Intimidating: Reprimands employees for the sake of a "tough guy" image.
• Judicial: Applies sound judgment.
• Promotional: Cultivates team spirit; rewards good work; encourages subordinates to realize their full potential.
• Secretive: Not open or outgoing in speech, activity, or purpose.

NOTE: These are a few easy points to pick up on the exam, but they can also be a few easy points to lose. They sound rather self-evident; they sound like they explain what they are but look at authoritarian. It does not necessarily mean that you are passing down many edicts. It gives specific guidance, expects adherence to rules and standards, and lets individuals know what is expected of them. It does not sound like a mean individual. An authoritarian sounds like somebody who is providing some measure of authority. Go through these and make sure you understand the true meaning behind each.

MANAGEMENT SKILLS

The Project Management Context section of the PMBOK Guide paragraph 2.4 focuses on the following general management skills:

- Leading: Establishing direction, aligning people, and motivating and inspiring.
- Communicating: The exchange of information, which has a variety of dimensions including written and oral, internal and external, formal and informal, as well as vertical and horizontal.
- Negotiating: Conferring with others in order to come to terms or reach an agreement; may focus on any or all of the following: scope, cost, and schedule objectives; changes; contract terms and conditions; assignments; or resources.
- Problem solving: A combination of problem definition and decision making.
- Influencing the organization: The ability to get things done, based on an understanding of the formal and informal structures of the organization.

PERFORMANCE REPORTING

Performance reporting is part of a project's communication system. The purpose of performance reporting is to collect and distribute information to project stakeholders about how effectively a project's resources are being used.

It is important to understand that performance reporting is not only a component of the communications variable, but also part of the fourth step of the project management process: controlling.

Performance reporting can affect project costs when time for writing the reports is not allocated in a project's schedule. The time spent writing the reports should be included as part of a project's costs. If the time is not recorded, then the project's total cost will be inaccurate. The time between one performance report and the next is called a reporting period. A reporting period might coincide with the beginning and end of a project phase.

When reporting periods do not coincide with project phases, it might be helpful to team members if the project manager includes dates for reporting periods on the project's schedule. Including reporting periods on the schedule helps team members know when they need to write performance reports. It includes:

- Status reporting
- Progress reporting
- Forecasting

A variety of techniques are used for performance reporting. Earned value analysis is important to performance reporting because it can give the project manager and team members the most accurate measure of whether or not a project's activities are being completed as planned. The most commonly used measures are the cost variance and the schedule variance. These two values can be converted to efficiency factors to reflect the project's cost and schedule performance. The cost performance index is the most commonly used cost-efficiency indicator, and the cumulative CPI is widely used to forecast project costs at completion.

Other tools and techniques for performance reporting include:

- **Performance reviews** - Performance reviews are meetings conducted to discuss a project's status. A project manager should hold performance reviews throughout the project to make sure team members and project activities are on track.
- **Variance analysis** - Variance analysis is used to gauge how closely a project adheres to its schedule, resource use, and budget provisions. Variance analysis can also be used to determine whether or not a project's quality standards are met.
- **Trend analysis** - Trend analysis is used to evaluate a project's progress over time. For example, trend analysis can be used to determine whether a solution to a problem is effective by looking at whether or not the problem still exists once a solution has been implemented. Trend analysis can also be used to show patterns of resource consumption across a project.

The following are common classifications of performance reports:

- **Routine** – Routine or regular, performance reports are not necessarily scheduled, but might be distributed at intervals that coincide with project phases or milestones. The frequency of performance reports depends on how smoothly the project is functioning.
- **Exception** – Exception performance reports provide project team members with information they need to make decisions or notify them of a change that affects their work. Exception performance reports are also distributed to stakeholders to inform them that a decision has been made.
- **Special Analysis** – Special analysis performance reports contain information about the results of a special study. Special studies might be conducted as part of a project or to determine a solution to a problem encountered during a project. Special analysis reports are useful not only to a current project, but are valuable documentation of lessons learned for future projects.

DOCUMENTATION

Good documentation is usually associated with successful projects. This is true regardless of the project's size. It is not acceptable to ignore documentation just because "the project is too small" to bother with it. Further, good documentation coupled with a disciplined change control process will go a long way toward reducing unauthorized changes in the scope of a project. PMI states that all documentation is produced to record and analyze project performance, including documents that describe the project's product, must be available for review during administrative closure.

There are two types of project documentation that PMI considers especially important in fostering good project communication:

- **Progress reports** - One of the most important ongoing components of effective project communication
- **Project plan** - The careful analysis required to document the project plan tends to reduce uncertainty on the project, and the distribution of the plan does a lot to keep appropriate people informed

ADMINISTRATIVE CLOSURE

Administrative closure, or concluding a project, is the formal process of verifying the completion of each project phase, and also completion of the project as a whole. Administrative closure involves confirming that the end product of a project satisfactorily meets the project's goals.

As part of administrative closure, a project manager and team members write detailed reports, also called close-out reports—about the processes used for phase and overall project completion, including any lessons learned during the project. Writing these reports helps the team evaluate how successfully they met the project's objectives. The reports are then archived for use as a reference for future projects.

It is important to understand that concluding a project is not only a component of the communications variable, but also part of the fifth step of the project management process: closing.

Close-out reporting is often neglected because concluding a project is not as exciting or interesting as beginning a project. The project manager or team members might not recognize the value of writing close-out reports, and they might become lazy. Also, team members are frequently eager to start a new project, so they start looking ahead instead of focusing on the present. It is important to complete close-out reports for every project. For example, close-out reports assure a project's stakeholders that the project is actually complete. As part of close-out reporting, a project manager should obtain signed confirmation from a project's key stakeholders to ensure their awareness of the project's status.

PMI states that each phase of the project should be closed so important and useful information is not lost. In addition, employee skills in the staff pool database should be updated to reflect new skills and proficiency increases.

Outputs from administrative closure include:

- <u>Project archives</u> - These include any project documents completed during the project process. PMI stresses the importance of paying special attention to archiving financial records when a project is completed under contract or involves significant procurement.
- <u>Project closure</u> - The project closure output relates to verifying that the product of the project meets all the requirements and obtains formal sign-off of the acceptance of the product. Formal acceptance also includes distributing notice of the acceptance of the project by the stakeholders or customers. Documenting formal acceptance is important because it signals the official closure of the project
- <u>Lessons learned</u> - Lessons learned are the final output of this process. The purpose of lessons learned is the same as we've seen elsewhere in this book. They're used to document the successes and failures of the project.

NOTE: Make sure you know the difference between administrative closure as discussed above and contract close-out as discussed in the Project Procurement Management section because certain versions of the exam have multiple questions in this area.

CHAPTER REVIEW

1. What process is communications planning often tightly linked with?
   A. Organizational planning
   B. Organizational development
   C. Information distribution
   D. Team development

2. _____ includes the processes required to ensure timely and appropriate generation, collection, dissemination, storage, and ultimate disposition of project information.
   A. Quality standards
   B. Process control
   C. Project quality control
   D. Project communication management

3. As a project manager, when communication is received from a subordinate in verbal form, you as the manager should generally respond in which of the following forms?
   A. Oral
   B. Written
   C. Formal
   D. Verbal

4. Which of the following is true regarding communication within a project environment?
   A. Effective meetings, a "war room," and a tight matrix promote effective communication
   B. Most project managers spend 60 percent of their time engaged in communication
   C. If a project consists of eight people, thirty-two potential channels of communication exist
   D. The project manager assumes the burden of project responsibility

5. What process consists of documenting project results to formalize acceptance of the product of the project by the sponsor or customer?
   A. Administrative closure
   B. Project close-out
   C. Phase termination
   D. Phase completion

6. _____ makes the needed information available to project stakeholders in a timely manner.
   A. Executive management updates
   B. Project status reports
   C. Information distribution
   D. Process control

7. Performance reporting tools and techniques include all of the following except:
   A. Variance analysis
   B. Scope analysis
   C. Trend analysis
   D. Performance reviews

8. Congratulations! You were just promoted to senior project manager and part of your new responsibilities is participating in performance reviews for all projects that last more than one year and cost more than $1 million. To prepare for these reviews and to ensure they are meaningful and can be used to determine future project direction, you believe project managers must ensure that:
   A. Earned value analysis is used for all projects.
   B. The focus is on cost and schedule variances rather than scope, resources, quality, and risks.
   C. All project documents are available to meeting attendees before the meeting.
   D. Accurate, uniform information about work results is provided.

9. Receivers in the communication model filter all their information through all of the following except?
   A. Culture
   B. Language
   C. Knowledge of the subject
   D. Conflict

10. As a skilled project manager you realize you can enhance project communications and team building by doing all the following except:
    A. Being a communication expeditor
    B. Having a "war room"
    C. Holding effective meetings
    D. Being a good communication blocker

11. In person-to-person communication, messages are sent on verbal levels and nonverbal levels hand signals and facial expressions simultaneously. What percentage of the message actually is sent through nonverbal cues?
    A. 20 to 30 percent
    B. 30 to 40 percent
    C. 40 to 50 percent
    D. Greater than 50 percent

12. As a project manager, you know that the process of conferring with other team members to reach an agreement or consensus is called:
    A. Win-win
    B. Negotiation
    C. Confrontation
    D. Resolution

13. Project information that may be distributed using a variety of methods including project meetings, hard-copy document distribution, shared access to networked electronic databases, fax, electronic mail, voice mail, and video conferencing is called:
    A. Project controls
    B. Project Information Management System (PIMS)
    C. Informational distribution systems
    D. Project distribution systems

14. Performance reports provide information to stakeholders on project scope, schedule, cost, and quality. Which of the following is most accurate when describing this process?
    A. Performance reporting shows network dependencies and relationships
    B. Performance reporting includes status reports, which detail where the project is now; progress reports, which describe accomplishments; and forecasts, which predict future status and progress
    C. The configuration control board receives performance reports and generates change requests to modify aspects of the project
    D. Performance reporting focuses on examining earned value analysis to determine budget updates

15. You are senior on a project that had four project team members and just added three additional members to your team. How many additional communication channels do you now have?
    A. 18
    B. 21
    C. 13
    D. 15

16. As project manager, you know that administrative closure should not be delayed until project completion because:
    A. The project manager may be reassigned
    B. Sellers are anxious for project
    C. Team members will be reassigned
    D. Useful project information may be lost

17. As director of the project management office you are explaining to your project managers that ideally, communication between the project manager and the project team members should take place
    A. Through approved template forms
    B. Via daily or weekly status reports
    C. Through the formal chain of command
    D. By written and oral communication

18. The process of performance reporting includes all of the following except:
    A. Progress reporting
    B. Status reporting
    C. Product analysis
    D. Forecasting

19. According to what you have learned on the job, contract closeout is similar to administrative closure in that the both involve which of the following?
    A. Product verification
    B. Project verification
    C. Quality assurance measures
    D. Scope modification measures

20. The act of moving information from you the project manager (sender) to a team member (receiver) is called
    A. Networking
    B. Functioning
    C. Transmitting
    D. Communicating

ANSWERS

1. A
2. D
3. A
4. A
5. A
6. C
7. B
8. D
9. D
10. D
11. D
12. B
13. C
14. B
15. D
16. D
17. D
18. C
19. A
20. C

PROJECT RISK MANAGEMENT

Most people find the Project Risk Management questions on the exam demanding because they address many concepts that some project managers have not been exposed to in their work or education. However, the questions correspond closely to the PMBOK Guide material so you should not have much difficulty if you study the concepts and terminology found in the PMBOK Guide. Although the questions included do not contain mathematically complex work problems, they do require you to know certain theories, such as expected monetary value (EMV) and decision-tree analysis. Additionally, you are likely to encounter questions related to levels of risk faced by both buyer and seller based on various types of contacts.

PMI views risk management as a four-step process including risk identification, risk quantification, risk response development, and risk control. PMBOK Guide figure 11.1 provides an overview of this approach.

Project Risk Management contains six processes: Risk Management Planning, Risk Identification, Qualitative Risk Analysis, Quantitative Risk Analysis, Risk Response Planning, and Risk Monitoring and Control.

As the name of this knowledge area implies, these processes are concerned with identifying and planning for potential risks that may impact the project. Organizations will often combine several of these processes into one step. The important thing about this process is that you should strive to identify all the risks and develop responses for those with the greatest consequences to the project objectives.

In order to manage project risk, you must first understand what constitutes risk. First, risks are generally associated with uncertain outcomes or a lack of knowledge of future events. Second, risks are measured according to the probability of their occurrence and the consequences of not achieving project goals. Finally, project risk compares actual project and product results to the project's quality standards. Know the concept of risk versus reward.

TYPES OF RISK

Project risk includes both threats to the project's objectives and opportunities to improve on those objectives. A risk has a cause, and if it occurs, a consequence. There are two broad categories of risk:

- Known risks - situations that the project team is certain will occur and can manage.
- Unknown risks - situations that cannot be anticipated, or managed and controlled directly. For example, a fire might burn down the factory that is supplying all of the resources for your project.

THERE ARE TWO MAIN TYPES OF RISK:

- <u>Business risks</u>: Normal risks of doing business that carries opportunities for both gain and loss.
- <u>Pure or insurable risks</u>: Those risks that present only an opportunity for loss. They are divided into four categories:
    1. Direct property damage (including automobile—related risks)
    2. Indirect consequential loss (business interruptions, costs to clean up after a loss, and so on)
    3. Legal liability
    4. Personnel

NOTE: The assumption is that you need not actively manage pure risk if you can insure against it; insurance is a type of risk transfer. You, therefore, focus your efforts on the business risk that may affect the organization.

RISK FACTORS

Risk factors are characterized as follows:

- Risk event: precisely what might happen to the detriment of the project
- Risk probability. how likely the event is to occur
- Amount at stake: the extent of loss or gain that could result

NOTE: As you read through this area, pay special attention to the questions: What is risk management?, And what are the types of risk? Know the difference between a pure and a business risk. Using the analogy of an auto accident, the risk for you, as the driver, is generally a pure risk; you only have the opportunity for loss. However, the risk for your insurance company is a business risk. It is part of that company's opportunity for gain or loss whenever they do business.

PMI argues that you do not really have to deal with pure risks; you can insure those away on your project. You may say, "I cannot afford to insure them." It does not matter. For the PMP exam, you need to know that you generally do not worry about managing the pure risks.

You need to know the factors of risk. Every risk consists of an event, a probability, and an amount at stake. You need to ask yourself: What bad things can happen during this event? What are the odds that this bad thing is going to happen? In addition, how much is it going to cost me if it does happen?

Finally, for this section, you need to know process identification, quantification, risk response development, and risk response control.

RISK PROCESSES

The remainder of the review focuses on the key points of PMI's approach to risk management, which include the six major risk processes (PMBOK Guide figure 11.1):

- Risk management planning
- Risk identification
- Qualitative risk analysis
- Quantitative risk analysis
- Risk response planning
- Risk monitoring and control

RISK MANAGEMENT PLANNING

Risk management planning must be done during the whole life of the project. In the beginning of the conceptual stage of the project, risks are identified almost without effort as the different aspects of the project. It is important that when these risks are thought of, they are recorded and placed in a risk management file or folder so that they can be dealt with later in the project.

As time goes by and progress is made on the project, the risks need to be reviewed, and the identification process must be repeated for the discovery of new risks. This must be an ongoing, continuous process. Risks that are identified early in the project may change as time goes by. As the project advances, some risks will disappear and other risks that were not thought of earlier will be discovered. As the possibility of the risk approaches, the risk needs to be reevaluated to be sure that the assessment of the risk made earlier is still valid.

The output of this process is the project's risk management plan, which is prepared with the assistance of the project manager, project team leaders, and other key stakeholders as needed. The plan may include:

- Risk management methodology
- Roles and responsibilities of team members
- Risk budget
- Schedule of risk management activities
- Risk threshold criteria
- Risk documentation procedures
- Risk audit schedule

RISK IDENTIFICATION

Risk identification involves recognizing and classifying all of the areas of potential risk related to a project. The attention to detail used when performing risk identification determines how effectively project risks can be managed. This process involves identifying three related factors: (1) potential sources of risk, (2) possible risk events, and (3) risk symptoms.

The timing of risk identification is also important. PMI advocated that risk identification should first be accomplished at the outset of the project and then updated regularly throughout the project life cycle. It is an iterative process.

The PMBOK Guide describes a number of useful inputs to the risk identification process, including the following:

RISK CATEGORIES
Having risk categories, such as those that follow, facilitates the identification of risk:

- Technical, quality, or performance risks
- Project management risks
- Organizational risks
- External risks

OTHER SOURCES OF RISK IDENTIFICATION

- Historical information on prior projects
- Output from other planning processes that identifies risks across the project, including the following:

WORK BREAKDOWN STRUCTURE
The WBS identifies all the work that must be accomplished, and it can provide a very useful structure for considering potential sources of project risk. PMI does recognize, however, that not all project risks can be identified using the WBS alone.

STAFFING PLAN
Do the human resource issues of the project pose any concerns or opportunities? For example, are any unique skills required that might be expensive or difficult to replace?

PROCUREMENT MANAGEMENT PLAN
Perhaps a sluggish local economy offers opportunities to reduce contract costs. Perhaps there is only one supplier available for a key component, thereby posing a subcontractor risk and possibly raising the price for that item.

SEVEN RISK IDENTIFICATION TOOLS AND TECHNIQUES

1 **Brainstorming** - This is probably the most used technique in the risk identification process. Its goal is to obtain a comprehensive list of potential risks that can be addressed later in the risk process. Brainstorming is useful in generating any kind of list by pulling out the ideas and thoughts of the participants. After the brainstorming process, risks are categorized by type, and their definitions are sharpened.

2 **Delphi method** - This method relies on gathering expert opinions through the following process. A group of experts are asked to provide answers to a list of questions. The experts work individually and are often not even physically present in the same location.

The answers from all the experts are combined and summarized, and the information is provided to everyone. The process is repeated until some reasonable consensus emerges from the group. Historical experience has shown that some degree of consensus usually emerges after about three rounds.

3   **Interviews** - The person responsible for risk identification identifies the appropriate individuals, briefs them on the project, and provides background information such as the WBS and any assumptions. Interviewees then identify risks based on their experience, project information, and other sources they may find useful.

4   **SWOT analysis** - A strengths, weaknesses, opportunities, and threats (SWOT) analysis also may be conducted to increase the breadth of risks considered.

5   **Checklists** - These can be developed based on historical information and knowledge from previous projects. Be aware of the advantages of checklists (quick and simple) and disadvantages (it is impossible to ensure all risks are covered in the checklist and it may limit its users). Take care to explore items on the checklist before using it to make sure the checklist is relevant for the specific project. Also note that if checklists are used, they should be reviewed and updated as appropriate during the closing stages of the project.

6   **Assumption analysis** - Explores the validity of the assumptions on which the project is based.

7   **Diagramming techniques** - Cause-and-effect or fishbone diagrams and system or process flowcharts were discussed in Chapter 6. Influence diagrams that show graphically causal influences, time ordering of events, or other relationships among variables and outcomes also can be used.

RISK IDENTIFICATION OUTPUT

A list of risks is the output of the process. Risk triggers (also known as symptoms or warning signs) also are outputs. They are indirect manifestations of actual risk events. For example, poor morale may be an early warning of significant schedule delay.

NOTE: Here is a trick that may help you. PMI argues that risk identification should first be accomplished at the outset of the project. So you may run into a question that asks, when should we first do risk identification? The answer is, throughout the entire project. Good project managers do risk identification constantly. However if the question is phrased as, when should we first do risk identification? The answer is, at the concept phase, at the very beginning of the project.

QUALITATIVE RISK ANALYSIS

Qualitative risk analysis involves determining what impact the identified risks will have on the project and the probability they'll occur. It also puts the risk in priority order according to their effect on the project objectives. Qualitative risk analysis should be performed throughout the project. Using qualitative methods will allow you to determine the probability that a risk will occur and to evaluate its consequences. Most qualitative risk analysis methodologies make use of a number of interrelated elements:

THREATS - These are things that can go wrong or that can 'attack' the system. Examples might include fire or fraud. Threats are ever-present for every system.

VULNERABILITIES - These make a system more prone to "attack" by a threat or make an attack more likely to have some success or impact. For example, in the event of a fire, a vulnerability would be the presence of inflammable materials (e.g. paper).

CONTROLS - These are the countermeasures for vulnerabilities. There are four types:

- Deterrent controls reduce the likelihood of a deliberate attack
- Preventative controls protect vulnerabilities and make an attack unsuccessful or reduce its impact
- Corrective controls reduce the effect of an attack
- Detective controls discover attacks and trigger preventative or corrective controls.

It can lead to further quantitative risk analysis or directly to risk responses, and it should be performed throughout the project.

PROBABILITY/IMPACT RISK RATING MATRIX

PMI suggests that a probability/impact risk rating matrix be constructed to assign a risk rating such as very low, low, moderate, high, and very high to risks and risk conditions based on combining probability and impact scales. A risk's probability scale falls between 0.0 or no probability to 1.0 or certainty. The impact scale reflects the impact of the risk on the project objectives. The intent is to assign a relative value to the impact on the project objectives if the risk occurs. The probability/impact matrix is a common way to combine two dimensions to determine whether a risk is considered very low, low, moderate, or high. The risk score or risk exposure helps put the risk into a category that will guide risk response actions.

IMPACT ANALYSIS

Impact analysis is a simple tool used to determine the trade-off for each possible risk event: What is the likelihood that the event will occur versus the severity of the impact on the project if it does occur? It is an easy task to plot each risk event on a graph showing this trade-off. In this way, it is possible to discern whether the project has mostly low probability—low impact risk events or some other combination.

DATA PRECISION RANKING

Data precision ranking is a technique employed to qualify risks and is, therefore, useful for risk management.

QUALITATIVE RISK ANALYSIS OUTPUT

- Overall risk ranking for the project
- List of prioritized risks with significant risks having a description of the basis for the assessed probability and impact
- List of risks that would be prime candidates for more analysis and risk management actions
- Trends in qualitative risk analysis results to determine whether risk response or further analysis is more or less urgent and important (PMBOK Guide paragraph 11.3.3.4)

QUANTITATIVE RISK ANALYSIS

Quantitative risk analysis looks at the risks you've identified and assigns numeric probabilities to each risk. It examines each risk and its potential impact on the project objectives, and evaluates the impacts of risk and quantifies the risk exposure of the project. It determines any interactions among the risks and assesses the range of potential outcomes. Risk quantification essentially helps in comparing and evaluating options in order to:

- Determine the probability of achieving a project objective
- Quantify the risk exposure for the project, and determine the size of cost and schedule contingency reserves that may be needed
- Identify risks requiring the most attention by quantifying their relative contribution to project risk
- Identify realistic and achievable cost, schedule, or scope targets

NOTE: You will be heavily tested on the common tools used for quantifying risk. You do not have to perform any complex calculations; however, you must be familiar with the concepts as presented in the PMBOK Guide and in the following review.

INTERVIEWING

Continuous probability distributions are typically used in quantitative risk analysis. If triangular distributions are used, information would be gathered on the optimistic (low), pessimistic (high), and most likely scenarios or on mean and standard deviation if a normal or log normal distribution is used.

SENSITIVITY ANALYSIS

Sensitivity analysis is a quantitative method of analyzing the potential impact of risk events on the project. Sensitivity analysis can also be used to determine stakeholder risk tolerance levels.

STATISTICAL INDEPENDENCE

The concept of statistical independence is a necessary condition for the use of tools such as expected value and decision-tree analysis. A practical definition of statistical independence is that two events are said to be independent if the occurrence of one is not related to the occurrence of the other.

If events are occurring at random, they are independent; if events are not occurring at random, they are not independent. A set or group of possible events are said to be mutually exclusive and collectively exhaustive if they are all independent, and the sum of their probabilities of occurrence is 1.0. This is the basic notion behind expected value.

DECISION-TREE ANALYSIS

This notion of expected value is a prerequisite to the following discussion on decision-tree analysis. Decision-tree analysis attempts to break down a series of events into smaller, simpler, and more manageable segments. Many similarities exist between decision-tree analysis and more complicated forms of management and risk analysis, such as PERT and CPM. All three forms of analysis presume that a sequence of events can be broken down into smaller and smaller segments, to more accurately represent reality.

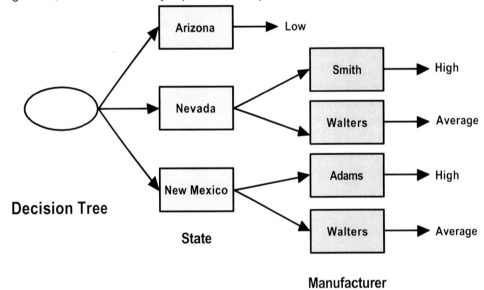

DECISION-TREE ANALYSIS GUIDELINES

- A box represents a decision; circles represent events with multiple possible outcomes.
- The primary decision (root decision) you are evaluating is placed at the left side of the decision tree, and the tree is drawn from that root.
- Find the most advantageous path at each decision node (box). What makes a path advantageous—lowest cost, greatest return, and so on depends on the specific situation.
- Draw all possible paths for the scenario.

- Place dollar values on each path segment if appropriate.
- Place probabilities on the path segments leading from events. Decision nodes have no probabilities associated with their alternatives.
- Determine the risk values for each path segment by multiplying all probabilities to the left of the segment (including any probability for the segment itself) by each other and then by the dollar value of the segment (if any).
- For each decision node, determine the most advantageous path by adding the risk values for the alternatives. You must work from right to left. Determine the paths for the rightmost decision nodes, and then work
- Your way to the left. The reason for choosing one path is that the paths are mutually exclusive; you can only choose one path.
- For event nodes, consider each path and add the results. The reason for including all paths is that they are mutually inclusive; that is, together they form the entire universe of possible outcomes.
- Continue working to the left until you can determine the most advantageous path for your root decision.

MONTE CARLO ANALYSIS

The concept of simulation, typically using Monte Carlo analysis, is also tested. A project simulation uses a model that translates the uncertainties specified at a detailed level into their potential impact on objectives that are expressed at the total project level. One crucial point is that Monte Carlo analysis is considered a superior approach to analyzing the schedule when compared to PERT or CPM. This is true because PERT and CPM fail to account for path convergence and, as a result, tends to underestimate project durations. Another important point is that the choice of statistical distribution used in the Monte Carlo routine can have important effects on the results of the simulation. For a cost risk analysis, a simulation may use the traditional project WBS as its model.

QUANTITATIVE RISK ANALYSIS OUTPUT

Output from quantitative risk analysis includes the following:

- Prioritized list of quantified risks
- Estimate of time and cost, including associated confidence levels, of project performance
- Likelihood of meeting objectives
- Indication of the need to provide more or less risk management action

NOTE: When it comes to risk quantification, you are going to deal with the idea of statistical independence. That is, what risks do not relate to each other? Their probabilities do not change based on the occurrence of other risks. With statistical dependence one risk leads to another. That is when risks are statistically dependent.

For expected value understand that it is the probability multiplied by the impact. That is the basics of expected value. For example, there is a 10 percent probability that your car will be in an accident costing $10,000. Ten percent of $10,000 is $1,000. That is the expected monetary value of that accident.

Monte Carlo analysis and path convergence: Path convergence goes back to the issue of statistical dependence and independence. You have all three paths. All three paths in the network are critical. Draw three lines going into a single point. It could be the finish node of your project. You have three lines. The first line is a first path, and it has a probability of on-time completion of 40 percent. The second has path has probability of on-time completion of 40 percent. The third has a probability of on-time completion of 20 percent. What are the odds that you are going to complete those three paths, which are all critical, in time to bring in the project on time?

To do that you need to recognize that they are statistically dependent. All three have to be done on time for the project to be done on time. Thus, you multiply the probabilities: 40percent times 40 percent is 16 percent, and 20 percent of 16 percent is 0.032 or 3.2 percent. That means there is only a 3.2 percent probability that all three paths are going to get completed on time. That is the idea of path convergence, and it is generally applied when you do multiple simulations of a project.

UTILITY THEORY

Utility theory is an attempt to infer subjective value, or utility, from choices. Utility theory can be used in both decision making under risk (where the probabilities are explicitly given) and in decision making under uncertainty (where the probabilities are not explicitly given). Extensions of utility theory include subjective probability as well as distortions of probability. There are three traditions in utility theory. One attempts to describe people's utility functions and is called the descriptive approach. Another attempts to use utility in the construction of a rational model of decision making and is called the normative approach. The third attempts to bridge the descriptive and normative approaches by considering the limitations people have with the normative goal they would like to reach; this is called the prescriptive approach.

RISK RESPONSE PLANNING

Risk response planning consists of planning the appropriate actions for responding to project files. Once the project team determines that a risk warrants a response, they should develop a strategy to reduce the possible damage that the risk can cause. You should be especially familiar with the possible response strategies to threats, including

- Avoidance - Involves eliminating a specific threat by changing the project plan to eliminate the risk. It might be chosen if a particular risk event is simply unacceptable (for example, very high probability and severe consequence). A useful tool whenever this happens is to adopt an alternative strategy; that is, find another approach to get the job done.

- Transference - Passes the risk and the responsibility of developing a risk response to a third party. Note that this strategy does not eliminate the risk; it just gives another party responsibility for it.
- Mitigation - Specific actions are taken to reduce the probability and/or consequences of an adverse risk event to an acceptable level. For example, you might use proven technology to lessen technical, cost, or schedule risks; you could adopt less complex processes; or you could choose a more stable seller.
- Acceptance - A decision is made to accept the consequences. Acceptance can be active, for example, by developing a contingency plan to execute should the risk occur. Risk triggers should be defined and tracked. A fallback plan is developed if the risk has a high impact or if the selected strategy may not be fully effective. A contingency allowance or reserve, including amounts of time, money or resources to account for known risks, is the most usual risk acceptance response. Acceptance also may be passive, for example, by accepting a lower profit if some activities overrun.

RISK RESPONSE PLAN
The risk management response plan includes the following:

- Identified risks and their impact on the project
- A response plan for major risks
- The level of residual risk expected after the response plan is executed
- Contingency and fallback plans

RISK MONITORING AND CONTROL
Risk monitoring and control is the process of keeping track of all the identified risks and identifying new risks as their presence becomes known and residual risks that occur when the risk management plans are implemented on individual risks. The effectiveness of the risk management plan is evaluated on an ongoing basis throughout the project.

When a risk is apparently going to take place, the contingency plan is brought into place. If there is no contingency plan, then the risk is worked on an ad hoc basis using what is termed a workaround. A workaround is an unplanned response to a negative risk event.

The concern of the project manager and the project team is that the risk responses have been brought to bear on the risk as planned, that the risk response has been effective. Additional risks may develop, and additional responses may be necessary.

Risk management is a continuous process that takes place during the entire project from beginning to end. As the project progresses, the risks that have been identified are monitored and reassessed as the time that they can take place approaches. Early warning indicators are monitored to reassess the probability and impact of the risk. As the risk approaches, the risk strategies are reviewed for appropriateness, and additional responses are planned.

As each risk occurs and is dealt with, or is avoided, these changes must be documented. Good documentation ensures that risks of this type will be dealt with in a more effective way than before and that the next project manager will benefit from "lessons learned."

The major tools and techniques for risk monitoring and control include the following:

- Risk audits and reviews
- Earned value analysis
- Technical performance measurement

Principal output's from risk monitoring and control -

- Workaround plans or unplanned responses to emerging risks
- Corrective action, which consists of performing the contingency plan or workaround
- Updating the risk database to form the basis of a risk lessons learned program for the organization

CHAPTER REVIEW

1. Which of the following is not an objective of a risk audit?
    A. Confirming that the project is well managed and that the risks are being controlled
    B. Confirming that risk management has been practiced throughout the project life cycle
    C. Ensuring that each risk identified has a computed expected value
    D. Helping to identify the deterioration of the project's value potential in its early stages

2. Simulation uses a representation or model of a system to analyze the behavior or performance of the system. The results of a schedule simulation will not quantify the risk of which of the following:
    A. Different project strategies
    B. Different network paths
    C. Individual activities
    D. Risk management plan

3. Development as a team is critical to the project's ability to meet its objectives:
    A. True
    B. False

4. Using a contractor to perform a high-risk task is which form of risk response?
    A. Insurance
    B. Assumption
    C. Transference
    D. Mediation

5. The objective with which the project team will measure the effectiveness of its execution of the risk response plan is based on the?
    A. Risk assessment score
    B. Acceptable threshold for risk
    C. Overall risk ranking for the project
    D. Probability rating

6. As a project manager most of your statistical simulations of budgets, schedule, and resource allocations use which of the following approaches?
    A. AOA
    B. ADM
    C. Monte Carlo analysis
    D. Present value analysis

7. Which of the following processes assess the likelihood of risk occurrences and their consequences using numeric probability assignments?
   A. Qualitative risk analysis
   B. Quantitative risk analysis
   C. Risk identification
   D. Risk response planning

8. According to what you know as a project manager, risk mitigation could involve which of the following:
   A. A policy response system
   B. Purchasing insurance
   C. Corrective action
   D. Eliminating risk through quality assurance

9. Risk identification outputs include the following except:
   A. Risk triggers
   B. Decision trees
   C. Inputs to other processes
   D. Risk events

10. Accordingly, risk score measures the:
    A. Product of the probability and impact of the risk
    B. Reduced monetary value of the risk event
    C. Range of schedule and cost outcomes
    D. Variability of the estimate

11. In your company, you use the Delphi technique for identifying risks. You are explaining to new team members that it is important because it:
    A. Reduces bias in the analysis and keeps any one person from having undue influence on the outcome
    B. Presents a sequence of decision choices graphically to decision makers
    C. Defines the probability of occurrence of specific variables
    D. Takes into account the attitude of the decision maker toward risk

12. In your company, you have come to learn that a workaround is:
    A. An unplanned response to a negative risk event
    B. A plan of action to follow when a risk suddenly occurs
    C. A specific response to certain types of risk
    D. A reactive approach of responding to risks

13. What document outlines the action steps to be taken if an identified risk event should occur?
    A. Risk management plan
    B. Project plan
    C. Corrective action plan
    D. Contingency plan

14. Company "A," which is highly profitable, is willing to spend $250,000 to develop a proposal for a $1 billion contract; Company "B," which is operating at break-even, is not. This is defined as:
    A. Sources of risk
    B. Potential risk events
    C. Stakeholder risk tolerances
    D. Expected monetary value

15. Contingency planning involves
    A. Establishing a management reserve to cover unplanned scope changes
    B. Determining adjustments that will be needed during the implementation phase
    C. Preparing a separate document that will detail an alternate project plan
    D. Defining the steps to be taken if an identified risk event should occur

16. According to your readings in the PMBOK Guide risk mitigation involves
    A. Using performance and payment bonds
    B. Eliminating a specific threat by eliminating the cause
    C. Avoiding the schedule risk inherent in the project
    D. Reducing the expected monetary value of a risk event by reducing the probability of occurrence

17. Which of the following is the simplest form of risk analysis?
    A. Probability analysis
    B. Sensitivity analysis
    C. Delphi technique
    D. Utility theory

18. One of the risks your team has discovered is a high probability that the equipment you are developing will not perform under the pressure it needs to in the workplace. In order to handle this risk, you have chosen to prototype the equipment. This is an example of risk:

    A. Mitigation
    B. Avoidance
    C. Transference
    D. Acceptance

19. Which of the following processes is used in risk management to determine which risks might affect the project and documenting their characteristics?
    - A. Risk qualitative analysis
    - B. Risk identification
    - C. Risk response planning
    - D. Risk management planning

20. As manager of your company's project office, you must decide which projects will receive additional resources. You also decide which projects should be initiated, continued, or cancelled. One of the way's you make these decisions is to:
    - A. Assess trends in quantitative risk analysis results
    - B. Determine an overall risk ranking for the project
    - C. Assess trends in qualitative risk analysis results
    - D. Prioritize risks and conditions

ANSWERS

1. C
2. D
3. A
4. C
5. B
6. C
7. B
8. B
9. B
10. A
11. A
12. A
13. D
14. C
15. D
16. D
17. B
18. A
19. B
20. B

PROJECT PROCUREMENT MANAGEMENT

11

The Project Procurement Management questions on the PMP exam tend to be more process oriented than legally focused. The exam requires you to know the differences between the two categories of contracts (fixed-price and cost-reimbursement) and the risks inherent in each category for both the buyer and seller. Several questions will also test your knowledge of the various types of contracts within each category.

The processes in the Project Procurement Management knowledge area are as follows: Procurement Planning, Solicitation Planning, Solicitation, Source Selection, Contract Administration, and Contract Closeout.

Project procurement management is the process required to acquire the goods and services necessary to attain project scope. Goods and services typically are referred to as a product and are obtained from outside the performing organization.

PMI discusses Project Procurement Management from the perspective of the buyer in the buyer-seller relationship but notes that the buyer-seller relationship can exist at many levels on one project. On the exam the seller may be called a subcontractor, vendor, or supplier. The seller generally manages work as a project in and of itself. The buyer may also be referred to as the customer. The terms and conditions of the contract are a major input to the seller's processes. The terms and conditions may actually contain the input as it may describe key milestones, deliverables, or objectives, or they may serve as a constraint since they may limit the project team's options (for example, requiring buyer approval of staffing decisions or staffing changes).

PMI further discusses project procurement management from the perspective of the seller being external to the organization but notes that the discussion is also applicable to formal agreements entered into with other units in the performing organization. If informal agreements are used, then processes in Human Resource Management and Communications Management are more likely to apply. Apply extra caution when answering questions in this area: make sure you know whom the question refers to when you see the words buyer and seller. In most cases, the buyer is the project manager.

PROCUREMENT PLANNING

Procurement planning is a process of identifying what goods or services you are going to purchase from outside of the organization. Part of what you will accomplish in this process is determining whether you should purchase the goods or services at all, and if so, how much and when.

During this step, the project manager is responsible for describing the subcontract procurement need in terms of specification. Specification is a precise description of a physical item, procedure, service, or result for the purpose of purchase and/or implementation of an item or service.

NOTE: In addition to remembering the above definition of project procurement, you should also know who on the project team is primarily responsible for creating the project specification. The project manager is responsible for ensuring that the job gets done but must rely on the technical people to do the work.

- Drawings
- Delivery dates
- Estimated cost (the "independent estimate")

In identifying the need, the project manager also determines whether it is more advantageous to make or buy the needed item or service.

MAKE-OR-BUY ANALYSIS

Make-or-buy analysis is accomplished during the procurement planning phase (the first phase) in PMI's six-phase approach to procurement management. The purpose is to determine what to procure from outside the project team and when the procurement should occur. You should also be aware of the following key points:

- Make-or-buy analysis should consider both the direct as well as the indirect costs of a prospective procurement. In this context, PMI considers the indirect costs of buying an item from the outside to include the cost of managing and monitoring the purchasing process. Direct costs such as salaries of full-time project staff are incurred for the exclusive benefit of the project, whereas indirect costs or overhead costs such as executive salaries, insurance, and benefits are allocated to the project by the performing organization as a cost of doing business.
- Make-or-buy analysis should reflect the perspective of the performing organization as well as the project's immediate needs. For example, purchasing a capital item rather than renting or leasing it may not be cost effective.But if the performing organization has an ongoing need for the item, then the portion of the purchase cost allocated to the project may be less than the cost of the rental.

There are several possible decisions that might result from the make-or-buy analysis:

- Procure all or virtually all of the goods and services from a single supplier or from multiple suppliers
- Procure a significant portion of the goods and services from a single supplier or from multiple suppliers

- Procure a relatively minor portion of the goods and services from outside sources (single or multiple suppliers)
- Make everything in house; procure nothing from the outside

Key deliverables (outputs) produced include a procurement management plan and a statement of work (SOW). The procurement management plan is a subsidiary element of the project plan and includes such information as follows:

- The type of contract to be used
- The need for independent estimates
- The roles and responsibilities of the organization's procurement department and the project management team
- Where standardized procurement documents are located
- Multiple-vendor management techniques
- How procurement will be integrated into the project life cycle

The SOW describes the procurement item in sufficient detail so that prospective sellers can determine whether they are capable of providing the item. It is a narrative description of the products or services to be supplied under contract.

If the procurement item is presented as a problem to be solved, the SOW may be called a statement of objectives (SOO). Although the SOW is prepared during procurement planning, it may be revised and refined as it moves through the procurement process. Each individual procurement item requires a separate statement of work, but multiple products or services may be grouped as one procurement item in a single SOW. It is important that the SOW be as clear, complete, and concise as possible.

CONTRACT CATEGORIES AND RISKS

PMI places a great deal of emphasis on types of contracts and the assignment of risk between buyer and seller. Contract type selection is a tool and technique in procurement planning. The buyer's objective is to place maximum performance risk on the seller while maintaining incentive for economical and efficient performance. The seller's objective is to minimize risk while maximizing profit potential.

PMI recognizes three broad categories of contracts: fixed-price or lump-sum contracts, costs-reimbursement contracts, and time-and-materials (T&M) contracts. They are defined as follows:

FIXED-PRICE OR LUMP-SUM

These contracts set a specific, firm price for the goods and/or services rendered. The buyer and seller agree on a well-defined deliverable for a set price. In this kind of contract, the biggest risk is borne by the seller. Fixed price contracts are usually used for projects that will take a long time to complete and have a high value to the company.

COST-REIMBURSEMENT

These types of contracts are as the name implies. The costs associated with producing the goods or services are charged to the buyer. All of the costs the seller takes on during the project are charged back to the buyer, thus the seller is reimbursed. Cost reimbursable contracts carry the highest risk to the buyer, as the total costs are uncertain.

TIME-AND-MATERIALS (T&M)

Time and materials contracts are a cross between the fixed price and cost reimbursable contract. The full amount of the material costs is not known at the time the contract is awarded. This resembles a cost reimbursable contract, as the cost will continue to grow during the contract's life. The buyer assumes most of the risk in time and material contracts.

CONTRACT TYPES AND RISKS

Additionally, in Negotiating and Contracting for Project Management, PMI discusses the following five specific contract types.

1. Cost-plus-percentage-of-cost (CPPC) - A CPPC contract provides for the reimbursement of allowable costs of services performed plus an agreed-upon percentage of the estimated cost as profit. The seller is only obligated to make its best effort to fulfill the contract within the estimated amount; the buyer funds all overruns. This contract type is prohibited in U.S. federal contracting and is only rarely used in the commercial sector.

2. Cost-plus-fixed Fee (CPFF) - A CPFF contract provides for the reimbursement of allowable costs plus a fixed fee paid proportionately as the contract progresses. Although there is a ceiling on the seller's profit, there is no motivation to control costs. Therefore, most risk remains with the buyer. This contract type is used predominantly for research and development projects in which the effort required remains uncertain until the project is well under way.

3. Cost-plus-incentive Fee (CPIF) - A CPIF contract provides for the reimbursement of allowable costs plus a predetermined fee as a bonus for superior performance. If the actual cost is less than the expected cost, the buyer and seller share the savings, based on a predetermined formula. This contract type is used predominantly for projects with long performance periods and substantial hardware development and test requirements.

4. Fixed-price-plus-incentive Fee (FPI) - A FPI contract provides the seller with a fixed price plus a predetermined fee as a bonus for superior performance. The buyer and seller share the risk. This type of contract is used primarily for high-value projects involving long performance periods (for example, shipbuilding and major systems development projects).

5 Firm-fixed-price (FFP) - An FFP contract is a lump-sum contract under which the seller furnishes goods or services at a fixed price. The seller bears all risk, but is compensated with the greatest profit potential. This is the most common contract type, because it is best suited for situations with reasonably definite specifications and relatively certain costs.

NOTE: For the test know the following:

CPPC, CPFF, CPIF, FPI, FFP --- seller's risk moves from low to high

FFP, FPI, CPIF, CPFF, CPPC --- buyer's risk moves from low to high

CONTRACT INCENTIVES

Incentives in a contract provide a "carrot" for the contractor in an attempt to bring the objectives and interests of the contractor in line with those of the buyer. Experience has shown that contract incentives are indeed usually cost effective. Incentives can be structured in a variety of ways and are flexible in that they can be used in conjunction with any of the types of contracts identified by PMI.

NOTE: As you read through this information, make sure you recognize what role the project manager has in the process. When it comes to procurement planning, the project manager has a very large role. They are responsible for creating the project specification with our project team. Also be familiar with the make-or-buy analysis—should we actually do this ourselves or should we subcontract the work out?

Another key component of this is trying to determine what the appropriate contract type is for any given project. There are different weights on who is responsible and who is taking the risk associated with each type of contract. The seller takes the greatest risk in firm-fixed-price contracts. By contrast, the buyer is taking the lowest risk in a firm-fixed-price contract.

At the high end of the spectrum, the buyer takes the greatest risk in a cost-plus-percentage-of-cost contract. The lowest risk to the seller occurs in a cost-plus-percentage-of-cost contract. Those contracts are so advantageous to the seller that they are illegal in certain environments, including the United States Federal Government.

You should know the range of risk that goes between the contract types. It goes firm-fixed-price at the lowest, fixed-price-incentive fee is next, then cost-plus-incentive fee, cost-plus-fixed fee, and then finally, cost-plus-percentage-of-cost. That is the range from low risk to high risk for the buyer. By contrast that is the range from high risk to low risk for the seller, and you need to be aware of that dichotomy.

SOLICITATION PLANNING

Solicitation planning begins once a project manager has gone through the procurement planning process and decided that resources are needed from outside the project's parent company.

Solicitation refers to the project manager's search for contractors who can supply the resources needed for project completion.

A list of prospective contractors is a good starting point when deciding from which companies you want to procure project resources. Some companies keep lists of contractors they have used in the past. This list generally includes information about the contractors, such as what resources they provide, which contracts they have used and how successfully they fulfilled those contracts. This documentation is collectively called the "procurement documents," which is used to solicit proposals from prospective sellers. Procurement documents should be structured to facilitate accurate and complete responses from prospective sellers. The following should always be included with your procurement documents:

- Statement of Work
- A description of the desired form of response
- Required contractual provisions such as a copy of a model contract or nondisclosure provisions

CONTRACT ORIGINATION

To determine the type of procurement documents to develop, the contracting specialists survey potential sellers and originate either a unilateral or a bilateral contract. A contract, as defined by PMI, is a mutually binding agreement that obligates the seller to provide a specific product and obligates the buyer to pay for it. A contract is a legal relationship subject to remedy in the courts. A unilateral contract takes the form of a purchase order—a standardized form listing routine items at standard (for example, vendor catalog) prices. The seller usually accepts the purchase order automatically. Unilateral contracts issued in this way normally do not involve any negotiation and contain relatively low monetary amounts.

A bilateral contract is initiated through a request for quotations, request for proposals, or an invitation for bid. The choice of which bilateral method to use is guided by the following factors:

- An invitation for bid is usually appropriate for routine items when the primary objective is to find the best price. You must be able to clearly and accurately describe the items to be purchased. There are normally no negotiations and, although not an absolute requirement, the lowest bid usually wins.
- A request for quotations is used for relatively low monetary purchases of commodity items.
- A request for proposals is used for complex or nonstandard items of relatively high monetary value.

EVALUATION CRITERIA

An evaluation criterion refers to the method your organization will use to choose a vendor from the proposals you receive from the solicitation process. Scoring models might be used along with a rating model or system. Sometimes, the evaluation criteria are made public in the procurement process so that vendors know exactly what you are looking for. They may be objective, such as "a supplier needs to be ISO 9000 certified," or subjective, such as "the proposed supplier must have documented, previous experience with similar projects." When price is not the primary determinant of award, sellers may be evaluated by the following evaluation criteria:

- Understanding of product/project needs
- Technical proficiency

NOTE: As you read the PMBOK Guide and try to understand this section you really need to understand the differences in terms among invitations for bids, requests for quotations, and requests for proposals. You need to know what each is used for and how it is properly deployed. You also need to be aware that this is the responsibility of your procurement department. This is not the responsibility of the project manager.

SOLICITATION

This process involves obtaining bids and proposals from vendors in response to a request for proposal (RFP) and similar documents prepared during the solicitation planning process. The term often used to describe this process is source qualification, which is described as follows:

Working from internal files, qualified seller lists, trade journals, supplier catalogs, and industry contacts, contracting specialists develop a list of potential sellers. They then collect information on each potential seller's technical, manufacturing, financial, and managerial abilities to fulfill the potential contract. Conferences with prospective sellers are often held to ensure that they have a clear, common understanding of the procurement. Responses to questions must be incorporated into the procurement documents as amendments so all prospective sellers remain on equal standing. Advertising also is used to expand existing lists of potential sellers where appropriate. The project manager working with the contracting staff performs this function.

Proposals are the output from the solicitation process. Proposals are prepared by prospective sellers and describe the seller's ability and willingness to provide the required product or service. Proposals may be supplemented with an oral presentation.

SOURCE SELECTION

This process involves the receipt of bids or proposals and choosing a vendor to perform the work or supply the goods or services. The following questions can be helpful when evaluating proposals during solicitation and selection:

- Does the contractor understand the project's needs?
- Is the contractor capable of providing the required resources?
- What is the contractor's reputation?
- What is the price of the resource?

Based on the answers to those questions you may be able to compile a short list of qualified sellers.

EVALUATING PROSPECTIVE SELLERS

Various techniques are used for evaluating prospective sellers and they are not mutually exclusive. Many factors aside from cost and price may need to be evaluated. Price may be the primary determinant for an off-the-shelf item, but PMI notes that the lowest proposed price may not be the lowest cost if the seller proves unable to deliver the product in a timely manner. Proposals also often are separated into technical and price sections, and each may be evaluated separately. Evaluation criteria may include samples of the supplier's previously produced products or services to provide a way to evaluate its capabilities and the quality of its products. Suppliers may also include a review of past performance if they have worked with the contracting organization before. Several tools and techniques commonly used include:

- **Contract Negotiation -** Contract negotiation is an important part of the contract selection. During this process, the project manager bargains with a contractor to obtain project resources at a reasonable price. Once they reach an agreement, they negotiate the type of contract that will bind the agreement.
- **Weighting System -** A weighting system is an objective way to evaluate proposals and choose a contractor. When using a typical weighting system, a project manager assigns a numerical value to each evaluative criterion. Then, as the project manager reads the proposals, he can keep track of which proposals meet the criterion.
- **Screening System -** A screening system is another means of evaluating proposals and choosing a contractor. When using a screening system, a project manager sets minimum requirements for each evaluative criterion. If a proposal does not meet the minimum requirements, the project manager should reject the proposal.
- **Independent estimates -** The procurement department might conduct an independent estimate of the costs of the proposal and use this to compare to the vendor prices. If there are large differences between the independent estimate and the proposed vendor cost, one of two things is happening: 1) The statement of work, or the terms of the contract were not accurate enough to allow the vendor to come up with an accurate cost; or 2) the vendor failed to respond to all the requirements that were stated in the contract or in the statement of work.

NOTE: For the exam, know that using the PMP certification is an example of a screening system.

It is generally considered a good practice to ensure competition among a group of prospective sellers if possible. There is considerable literature documenting the benefits of competition. Why should we use a sole source?

- When a seller truly has a unique qualification that cannot be found or matched elsewhere.
- When other mechanisms exist to ensure that the price you are paying is reasonable. For example, you might have the in-house expertise to properly evaluate the seller's bid for reasonableness and accuracy.
- When your project is under extreme schedule pressure. Competitive contract selection almost always takes longer than noncompetitive contract selection because you must allow

time for preparing a solicitation document, for sending and receiving the solicitation, for the prospective sellers to prepare and submit a proposal, and for you to evaluate the proposals and make a selection.

CONTRACT NEGOTIATION STAGES AND TACTICS

According to PMI, contract negotiation consists of five stages:

- **Protocol** - Introductions are made and the atmosphere is set.
- **Probing** - Negotiators identify issues of concern, as well as the strengths and weaknesses of the other party.
- **Scratch Bargaining** - The actual bargaining occurs and concessions are made.
- **Closure** - Positions are summed up and final concessions are made.
- **Agreement** - The final agreement is documented.

In Negotiating and Contracting for Project Management PMI identifies the following negotiation tactics:

- **Deadline** - Imposing a deadline for reaching an agreement.
- **Surprise** - Taking the other party by surprise with new information.
- **Strategic Delay** - Requesting a recess to divert attention from the present discussion or to regroup.
- **Reasoning Together** - Collaborating to resolve problems for everyone's benefit.
- **Withdrawal** - Making a false attack on an issue and then retreating (to divert attention from a weakness).
- **Limited Authority** - Claiming inability to finalize the agreement just reached (a stalling tactic).
- **Missing Man** - Claiming that the person with final authority is absent.
- **Fair and Reasonable** - Offering comparisons to other situations, for example, to show that the price offered is reasonable.
- **Unreasonable** - Making the other party's request appear unreasonable.
- **Suggesting Arbitration** - Attempting to scare the other party into agreement.
- **Fait accompli** - Claiming that a topic of dispute has already been decided or accomplished and cannot be changed.

The project manager's negotiation objectives are to:

- Obtain a fair and reasonable price, while still getting the contract performed within certain time and performance limitations.
- Develop a good relationship with the seller. This objective cannot be overemphasized, because the buyer will pursue the relationship throughout the contract period.

The output from the source selection process is the contract. Contracts may be called an agreement, a subcontract, a purchase order, or a memorandum of understanding. Most organizations have documented policies and procedures that define who can sign such agreements on behalf of the organization, typically called a delegation of procurement authority.

As you look at this area, make sure you understand and recognize what terms are from the PMBOK Guide paragraph 12.4—contract negotiation, weighting system, screen system, and independent estimates.

Also, when it comes down to contract negotiation, make sure you know the five stages and what they mean. Protocol is rapport-setting; it is the handshake that goes on at the beginning of a contract negotiation. Probing is when you go out and try to investigate what is going on at the other side. Scratch bargaining is also known as hard-core bargaining, and you may see either term on the exam. Closure is when you come to an end, and agreement is when there are actual signatures on a piece of paper.

Also, be aware of the negotiation tactics of deadline and surprise. One that shows up more often than any other on the exam is fait accompli, which means claiming it is a done deal, claiming that it has already been agreed to.

CONTRACT ADMINISTRATION

Contract administration is the formal verification that the contractor has fulfilled his contractual obligations. As part of contract administration, the project manager must make sure all project team members are aware of their responsibilities with regard to a contract..

During this step, the project manager—with help from the contracting specialists—monitors the seller's performance against the contract's specifications, performance standards, and terms and conditions. PMI emphasizes that the legal nature of the contractual arrangement makes it imperative that the project team be aware of the legal implications of actions taken during contract administration.

CONTRACT DOCUMENT

At a minimum, the following items are usually documented in the contract:

- Delivery schedule
- Payment schedule - method for determining the price
- Handling of changes
- Warranties, insurance, inspections
- Delays termination
- Subcontracts, performance bonds

Contracts may have specific terms or conditions for completion and closeout. You should be aware of these terms or conditions so that project closure is not held up because you overlooked an important detail.   If you are not administering the contract yourself, ask your contracts/procurement department if there are any special conditions that you should know about.

STANDARD CLAUSES

Also, the use of standard clauses is encouraged where possible because they are legally sufficient for most contractual situations and because they cost less (customized contract language takes time and can sometimes be expensive to develop).

The following is a brief description of clauses specifically addressed in PMI's Contract Administration for the Project Manager.

CHANGES

- Changes to project scope constitute one of the major areas of cost growth
- Control of change
- Who initiates a change request
- How change is funded
- Final approval authority
- Configuration control
- Do not price changes on a cost-plus basis; use lump-sum

WARRANTIES

- Establish a level of quality
- Express warranty: Contract explicitly states what the level of quality is
- Implied warranty: Contract describes "merchantability" or "fitness of use"

DOCTRINE OF WAIVER

- The relinquishing of one party's contract rights because of a lack of enforcement of those rights

DELAYS

- Who caused it
- Nature of the interruption
- Impact

BONDS

- Performance bond: Secures for the buyer the performance and fulfillment of the contract
- Payment bond: Guaranteed payment to subcontractors and laborers by the prime or the guarantor

BREACH

- Failure to perform a contractual obligation
- Measure for damage is the amount of loss sustained by an injured party
- Material breach: More serious than a contract breach

NONFAULTED PARTY DISCHARGED FROM ANY FURTHER OBLIGATIONS

For example, when a contract stipulates that time is of the essence, failure to perform within the allotted time constitutes material breach and the project manager will not be required to accept late performance.

ELEMENTS OF A LEGALLY ENFORCEABLE CONTRACT

Finally, you should be familiar with the elements of a legally valid (enforceable) contract:

- The agreement must be voluntary (there must be both an offer and an acceptance).
- The people signing must have the legal capacity to do so
- There must be sufficient cause to contract—"consideration" must be provided to both parties
- The contract must be for a legal purpose and must not violate public policy

NOTE: Some references state there are five elements of a legally enforceable contract citing "offer" and "acceptance" as two distinct elements

CHANGES AND CHANGE CONTROL

All contracts should define the process by which any changes to the contract (project) can be accommodated and should include the paperwork, tracking systems, and approvals necessary for authorizing changes. The system should cover who initiates a change request, how it is processed and funded, and who has the final approval authority. Changes made, whether they be approved or unapproved, must be reflected in the appropriate project documents.

UNDEFINED WORK

Undefined work becomes an issue when "time is of the essence." The parties would like to proceed with the project, but the price and other important terms and conditions of the contract have not been specified or agreed to.

This situation can arise either at the outset of a contractual relationship or as a result of significant changes to an ongoing contract. At the outset of a contract, a contractor will often proceed on the basis of a "letter contract," with the details to be worked out later. Obviously, a certain amount of trust exists in such a circumstance. When undefined work arises as a result of changes, contractors often proceed without a formal change order authorizing them to do so.

CONTRACT CLOSEOUT

Contract closeout is the formal verification that contractors have completely and successfully fulfilled their obligations to a project. During contract closeout, all paperwork and electronic files used during the project must be updated and filed in a database for future reference. Most often, the contract will specify how the contract and project should be closed.

Contract records are very important and include the contract itself and other relevant documentation such as progress reports, financial records, invoices, and payment records. These are often kept in a contract file, which should be part of the complete project file. The contract file is a complete set of index records.

Contract documentation is also important should a procurement audit be initiated. Such an audit is a structured review of the procurement process from procurement planning through contract administration. The purpose of the audit is to identify success and failures that warrant transfer to other procurement items on the current project or future projects.

The person or organization responsible for contract administration should provide the seller with formal written notice when the contract has been completed. The contract should define the requirements for formal acceptance.

NOTE: Contract closeout includes two important provisions: one is product verification, and the second is administrative closeout. We need to make sure we have given the customer everything that we contracted to provide. That is what product verification is all about. Administrative closeout is paperwork that deals with all the administrative work associated with ensuring that the contract is ended properly.

ORGANIZING FOR CONTRACT MANAGEMENT

According to PMI a company can assign project contracting responsibility in a centralized or decentralized manner.

CENTRALIZED CONTRACTING

With centralized contracting, a single function within the company is responsible for the entire contracting process for all projects. Contracting procedures typically are stringent and standardized. This form works best in functionally organized companies.

ADVANTAGES
- More economical.
- Easier to control overall contracting efforts.
- Higher degree of contracting specialization.
- Orders can be consolidated across several projects.

DISADVANTAGES

- The contracting office can become a bottleneck if several projects have heavy needs at once.
- Less attention is given to the special needs of individual projects.

DECENTRALIZED CONTRACTING

With decentralized contracting, each project manager controls the contracting process for his or her project. This form works best if companies follow the projectized organization

ADVANTAGES

- Project manager has more control
- Contracting personnel are more familiar with project needs
- More flexible and adaptable to project needs

DISADVANTAGES

- Duplication of contracting efforts across projects
- Higher costs
- No standard contracting policies

FORCE MAJEURE

Force Majeure literally means "greater force." These clauses excuse a party from liability if some unforeseen event beyond the control of that party prevents it from performing its obligations under the contract. Typically, force majeure clauses cover natural disasters or other "Acts of God," war, or the failure of third parties—such as suppliers and subcontractors—to perform their obligations to the contracting party. It is important to remember that force majeure clauses are intended to excuse a party only if the failure to perform could not be avoided by the exercise of due care by that party.

When negotiating force majeure clauses, make sure that the clause applies equally to all parties to the agreement—not just the licensor. Also, it is helpful if the clause sets forth some specific examples of acts that will excuse performance under the clause, such as wars, natural disasters, and other major events that are clearly outside a party's control. Inclusion of examples will help to make clear the parties' intent that such clauses are not intended to apply to excuse failures to perform for reasons within the control of the parties.

PRIVITY OF CONTRACT

Privity of contract is a legal term that recognizes that the contractual relationship exists between a buyer and its prime contractor. No contract exists between the buyer and the subcontractors, and it is legally improper for a buyer to bypass a contractor and deal directly with a subcontractor(s).

Beyond the legal issue, there are other reasons for a buyer to be cautious about dealing with subcontractors. In doing so, the buyer may inadvertently relieve the prime contractor of certain responsibilities. For example, if a buyer informs a subcontractor that things might work better if the subcontractor would "try the following approach . . ." and the subcontractor runs into trouble, the prime contractor may rightfully claim that the buyer's interference caused the problems.

FOREIGN CURRENCY EXCHANGE

Whenever the buyer and the seller operate in different countries, one typically difficult issue always arises regarding the potential effects of fluctuating exchange rates. PMI does not require you to know any complicated formulas or procedures for the exam. You must simply be aware that all contracts should set forth the process for dealing with exchange rate issues. On many projects, the parties attempt to develop a process for preventing unfair or unintended gain or loss by either party.

CHAPTER REVIEW

1. You are working at a construction site and can lease a drill rig for $3,000 per day. To purchase the item, the investment would cost $220,000 and the daily cost is $1,000. If the drill is needed for 150 days should it be leased or bought?
    A. Purchase it because it would save $80,000
    B. Purchase it because it would save $40,000
    C. Lease it, as it would save $40,000
    D. Lease it, as it would save $80,000

2. In an effort to assist in project management training you have decided to hire an outside instructor to help with instruction. Referring to the organizations project management methodology, your subcontracts department informed you that the following document must be prepared before starting the procurement:
    A. Statement of work
    B. Procurement management plan
    C. Procurement contract methodology
    D. Evaluation methodology

3. In some cases, contract termination refers to
    A. Contract closeout by mutual agreement
    B. Contract closeout by delivery of goods or services
    C. Contract closeout by successful performance
    D. Certification of receipt of final payment

4. During solicitation planning, the project team is responsible for
    A. Determining the make-or-buy decision
    B. Developing the procurement documents
    C. Specifying schedule parameters of the key deliverables
    D. Developing the specifications for the solicitation

5. Project procurement management is discussed from the perspective of all of the following except:
    A. Buyer
    B. Sub-contractor
    C. Vendor
    D. Client

The Project Management Professional (PMP®) Exam Guide

6. From what you remember an associate telling you, contract closeout and administrative closure are similar in that they both require:
   A. That the project manager manages the activities involved
   B. Verification that no errors occurred at any time while the work was being performed
   C. That a WBS be properly prepared
   D. Verification that the work was completed satisfactorily

7. Procurement planning is the process of identifying which project needs can best be met by procuring products or services outside the project organization. When should this effort be accomplished?
   A. After contract negotiation
   B. During the scope definition effort
   C. During the cost definition effort
   D. While creating the work breakdown structure

8. All of the following elements must be evident in a written contract for it to be legally enforceable except:
   A. Pricing structure
   B. Legal capacity
   C. Mutual structure
   D. Appropriate capacity

9. Which of the following statements is not true with regard to cost reimbursement contracts?
   A. The seller's interest in cost control diminishes
   B. The buyer bears the greater financial risk
   C. The buyers concern about the sellers performance increases
   D. Payment is based solely on the delivery of goods and services

10. As project manager you are explaining to your team that, according to PMBOK Guide, all of the following are tools and techniques used in contract administration except:
    A. Contract change control system
    B. Contract negotiation
    C. Payment system
    D. Performance reporting

11. According to the PMBOK Guide inputs to contract administration include all of the following except:
    A. Work results
    B. Change requests
    C. Market conditions
    D. Seller invoices

12. Payment bonds are sometimes required by contract and require certain actions. Payment bonds are specifically designed to ensure that the prime contractor provides payment of
    - A. Subcontractors insurance
    - B. Insurance premiums
    - C. Insurance for accidents caused
    - D. Subcontractors, laborers, and sellers of material

13. According to the PMBOK Guide all of the following are tools and techniques relating to the process of source selection except?
    - A. Screening system
    - B. Contract negotiation
    - C. Performance reports
    - D. Independent estimates

14. You are explaining to another project manager that requirements for inspection and acceptance are defined in which of the following items?
    - A. Procurement management plan
    - B. Project charter
    - C. Overall project plan
    - D. Contract

15. You are leading a PMP study group. Currently you are reviewing contract administration and realize that all of the following are inputs to the process except
    - A. Work results
    - B. Seller invoices
    - C. Scope changes
    - D. Contract

16. Buyers use a variety of methods to provide incentives to a seller to complete work early or within certain contractually specified periods. From the seller's perspective, liquidated damages are what form of incentive?
    - A. Positive
    - B. Negative
    - C. Nominal
    - D. Risk-prone

17. Contract administration outputs include all of the following except:
    - A. Correspondence
    - B. Contract changes
    - C. Payment requests
    - D. Statement of work updates

18. A narrative description of products or services to be supplied under contract is called
    A. A statement of work
    B. The Project Plan
    C. Conceptual estimate
    D. Preliminary estimate

19. Procurement planning should be accomplished during
    A. Scope definition
    B. Creation of work breakdown structure
    C. Scope initiation
    D. As part of solicitation

20. As the senior project manager, you have decided to make an immediate decision and award a contract to a contractor that has provided its services to your company occasionally in the past few years. This particular contractor has a great record and your relationship is excellent. Your current project, although somewhat different from previous projects, is somewhat similar to other work he has performed. In this situation, to minimize your risk you should award what type of contract?
    A. Fixed-price with economic price adjustment
    B. Fixed-price incentive
    C. Firm-fixed-price
    D. Cost-plus-award fee

ANSWERS

1. A
2. B
3. A
4. B
5. D
6. D
7. B
8. A
9. D
10. B
11. C
12. D
13. C
14. D
15. C
16. B
17. D
18. A
19. A
20. C

PROFESSIONAL RESPONSIBILITY

. . . .

12

As of July 1, 2001, the PMP Exam will include another "domain" (the current domains are Initiating, Planning, Executing, Controlling and Closing) called "Professional Responsibility." This is included to ensure individual integrity and professionalism by adhering to legal requirements and ethical standards in order to protect the community and all stakeholders. It will be approximately 14.5 percent of the exam, or twenty-nine questions.

Professional Responsibility will focus on the following tasks:

- Ensuring integrity and professionalism
- Contributing to the project management knowledge base
- Enhancing individual competence
- Balancing stakeholders' interests
- Interacting with team and stakeholders in a professional and cooperative manner
- Specific knowledge areas and skills have been identified in the Role Delineation Study for each of these tasks.

These questions will be based on situations or scenarios that require an understanding of the Project Management Professional Code of Conduct and the importance of professional ethics, awareness of legal issues, cultural sensitivity, and managing conflict of interest.

EXAMPLE OF PROFESSIONAL RESPONSIBILITY TOPICS

The project manager's job is to ensure individual integrity and professionalism. This task requires knowledge of legal requirements, ethical standards, and understanding community and stakeholder values. It also requires skill in exercising appropriate judgment.

Each of these items can be related to specific knowledge areas of the PMBOK Guide. For example, legal requirements can be related to the area of Project Procurement Management.

Ethical standards and stakeholder values can be associated with Human Resource Management and Communications Management.

The key is in understanding the relationship between the tasks identified in the Professional Responsibility Domain with the nine knowledge areas and the processes described in the PMBOK Guide.

ENSURE INTEGRITY AND PROFESSIONALISM

As a project manager, your primary professional responsibilty is to ensure integrity of the project management process that is outlined in the PMBOK Guide. This applies not only to the project and product, but also in your own conduct.

A project has integrity if its product is sound and can be used by the stakeholders. If you follow the PMBOK Guide and practice the proper project management processes you will help ensure that both the project and product will have integrity.

Personal integrity means adhering to the ethical code set forth by PMI and that you will adhere to the PMP Code of Professional Conduct. You should clearly understand this code because once you submit your application to PMI you are agreeing to adhere to this code. The Code of Conduct is as follows:

As a PMI Project Management Professional (PMP), I agree to support and adhere to the responsibilities described in the PMI PMP Code of Professional Conduct.

I. Responsibilities to the Profession

  A. Compliance with all organizational rules and policies

    1. Responsibility to provide accurate and truthful representations concerning all information directly or indirectly related to all aspects of the PMI Certification Program, including but not limited to the following: examination applications, test item banks, examinations, answer sheets, candidate information and PMI Continuing Certification Requirements Program reporting forms.

    2. Upon a reasonable and clear factual basis, responsibility to report possible violations of the PMP Code of Professional Conduct by individuals in the field of project management.

    3. Responsibility to cooperate with PMI concerning ethics violations and the collection of related information.

    4. Responsibility to disclose to clients, customers, owners or contractors, significant circumstances that could be construed as a conflict of interest or an appearance of impropriety.

  B. Candidate/Certificant Professional Practice

    1. Responsibility to provide accurate, truthful advertising and representations concerning qualifications, experience and performance of services.

    2. Responsibility to comply with laws, regulations and ethical standards governing professional practice in the state/province and/or country when providing project management services.

  C. Advancement of the Profession

    1. Responsibility to recognize and respect intellectual property developed or owned by others, and to otherwise act in an accurate, truthful and complete manner, including all activities related to professional work and research.

2. Responsibility to support and disseminate the PMP Code of Professional Conduct to other PMI certificants.

II. Responsibilities to the Customers and the Public

   A. Qualifications, experience and performance of professional services

    1. Responsibility to provide accurate and truthful representations to the public in advertising, public statements and in the preparation of estimates concerning costs, services and expected results.

    2. Responsibility to maintain and satisfy the scope and objectives of professional services, unless otherwise directed by the customer.

    3. Responsibility to maintain and respect the confidentiality of sensitive information obtained in the course of professional activities or otherwise where a clear obligation exists.

   B. Conflict of interest situations and other prohibited professional conduct

    1. Responsibility to ensure that a conflict of interest does not compromise legitimate interests of a client or customer, or influence/interfere with professional judgments.

    2. Responsibility to refrain from offering or accepting inappropriate payments, gifts or other forms of compensation for personal gain, unless in conformity with applicable laws or customs of the country where project management services are being provided.

Another important area discussed in the Professional Code of Professional Conduct is conflict of interest. A conflict of interest is when your personal interests are put above the interest of the project or your stakeholders. Although not always easy or clearly definable, you must put the interest of the project over your own interest. If a conflict of interest should arise from such things as membership association, vendor gifts, or undue stakeholder influence you must inform the project sponsor at once of the conflict, failure to do so could result in legal action from the stakeholder and loss of your PMP certification.

CONTRIBUTE TO KNOWLEDGE BASE

Contributing to the knowledge base is taking any opportunity available and helping educate or train others in the field about correct project management skills, techniques, and current project management practices. This includes not only team members, but also management and current stakeholders. Learn how to communicate and transfer knowledge effectively, as a coach and mentor, and to use available research strategies.

Part of your commitment to PMI is that you will stay current on project management practices, theories, and techniques. To do this effectively you should set up a network of other project management professionals in your area. The first place you may wish to visit is the local PMI Chapter in your state. (To find out more about this subject matter, please visit, http://www.pmi.org/info/GMC_ChaptersOverview.asp).

BALANCE STAKEHOLDERS INTEREST

As you are aware, projects are undertaken at the request of a stakeholder. Most often, these stakeholders will have different needs and interests, and your job as the project manager is to try to balance the needs of the stakeholders with the projects. To do this you will need to understand the various competing stakeholders' interests and needs. Not all stakeholders have the same knowledge or work in the same department; because of this, your stakeholders will have competing needs. An example is that one stakeholder may want a software application that is easy to install, while another wants a word processing program that has an expandable dictionary. As project manager, it is your job to balance the two.

You will need to comprehend certain conflict resolution techniques in order to handle differing objectives. You need to remember to be fair in resolving conflicts during this period; the idea is to come up with a solution that is win-win for all parties involved.

INTERACT WITH TEAM AND STAKEHOLDERS

As the project manager you are the so-called "ring leader" and must learn to interact with the team members and stakeholders in a professional and cooperative manner. You need to also understand cultural diversity and make sure that your team members also understand this diversity. You must be able to show flexibility toward diversity, tolerance, and self-control.

More and more projects and project managers are working in a global situation. It is important to understand and respect that cultural differences do exist and not to impose your beliefs onto others. Realize that when you or your team members are working overseas that culture shock does occur. This can be true if you or your team goes overseas or if you have overseas visitors working in your office. Training and education are both good ways to provide information on cultural differences. It is extremely important to take the time to build solid relationships with others. Once a feeling of trust is established, the project planning process will go much smoother.

DEFINING CULTURE AND ITS NORMS

We define culture in as general terms as possible because culture is so broad and encompassing. It is simply everything human that a group shares among its members. It includes thought processes, belief systems, rules for behavior, rules governing families and marriage, and how one should set priorities—me first or the group first. It can make a project very successful or doom it despite all other reasons for success.

Every culture faces the same common problems. It is how cultures approach and solve these problems (food, shelter, marriage, communication, government, trade) that make them different from each other. Many of the outward actions that we see are based on internal values we do not see, but are part of the psyche of the person we are communicating with across a cultural divide. We can see and experience a foreign language, music, costumes, and folk stories. The values that underlie these require much greater study and where the majority of friction often exists in international projects.

Study of culture is possible because every culture must be learned by its members. Everything from language to etiquette to beliefs and values are learned from childhood. Cultures are not static—they constantly react to changes around them and are impacted, in both good and bad ways, by this change. Even within single countries we find multiple cultures that vary from the stereotype that foreigners expect to find upon arrival.

Culture must be learned and we can therefore learn multiple cultures if we apply ourselves to that endeavor. But why bother? The reason is simply economics. The global network is already upon us and the successful projects will involve those who can adjust and make things happen globally.

A first step to understanding other cultures is to understand your own. You must understand your own background and realize your own biases to be able to overcome them. The second step is to realize there are no good or bad cultures—only different ones. In fact, cultures are constantly learning and borrowing from each other ideas created in foreign cultures. Due to international exposure, your project will, most likely, find solutions to problems that can be adopted for all future projects.

CONSIDER WHEN YOU GOT UP THIS MORNING

Shaving first (a practice created in India and considered by other cultures as a very strange masochistic act), you then dress choosing a shirt made from Egyptian cotton that is one of your favorites. Your shoes and belt were made in Mexico. Maybe you probably had coffee, from Latin America, or chose tea, from China, while you watched for reports on traffic on a television made outside the United States.

Later, you heard news reports broadcasting live from around the world—something that your parents would have considered science fiction only decades earlier. You may have many friends living abroad that you have met, either physically or virtually on the 'Net, so news in those locations prick your interest. You don't realize that you know many more people outside your town than in your own neighborhood.

Then you probably drove to work—most likely in a car manufactured by a foreign manufacturer or comprised of foreign parts (at least you know your tires were made in Japan). Or maybe you took a train that was manufactured in Germany or Austria. You pass billboards advertising new products by company names you might have problems pronouncing, but you understand the products and think about buying them regardless. The Czech crystal looks especially nice with Christmas, a celebration of a religion originating in the Middle East, is just around the corner. As you pass the airport, an aircraft manufactured in France, flown by a foreign airline, and arriving from a Canadian airport lands right on schedule.

While at work, you spend the morning reading emails from foreign offices that are now closed. With these updates you talk long distance to foreign suppliers about a change predicted and an existing order that will need adjusting. During lunch, you choose to eat at a restaurant that specialized in Italian food that you love and have adopted as a regular practice. In the afternoon, you update your project files and send out new tasks to your team in India and Singapore, knowing that they will receive and complete them later while you are sleeping.

After work, you pick up your children at school and go straight to their soccer practice, a fairly recent cultural adoption of a traditionally European sport. Your children's heroes are soccer stars from foreign countries, while you still follow tennis. Every year, you watch the big matches such as Wimbledon in England. On the way home, you pick up some take-out from a Chinese restaurant. You opt for chopsticks and show your kids how to use them successfully during dinner at home.

You spend the evening watching a travel show about the best beaches in the world that gets you thinking about a vacation with your wife reminding you she wants to vacation someplace where she can get a tan. She has a professional conference coming up soon in Acapulco or maybe another trip to the Caribbean. You explore the currency exchange rates on the Internet to come with some ideas. Then you check a Web site about international trade conferences that coming up soon. Comments from different sides' debate the impacts of new deals speculated. You make a couple of notes of things to look into tomorrow at work—the possibility of impacts on your domestic operations and on your exports.

Then you help with homework over math (using Arabic numerals we take for granted) and history lessons about wars where cultures came into conflict in centuries past. Some issues seem to be the same as today; the problems were never solved. Later, you read your youngest child a bedtime story from an old fairy tale that originated in Germany.

Before going to bed, you brush your teeth with a toothbrush made in China, wash your face with soap made in France, and put on silk pajamas you bought a few years ago when on business in Japan.

Face it, this is not the same world that your parents grew up in—and it won't be the same world next year.

CULTURAL VALUES

A culture develops values based upon common factors of:

- Environment - defeat nature or surrender to nature as a supreme force
- Time - focused on task accomplishments or on relationships
- Action - rapid decisions and action or contemplation forecasting all impacts carefully before proceeding
- Communication - direct or indirect, formal or informal, low content (just the facts!) or high content that requires emotion and personal contact to deliver the message as intended
- Space (personal versus public) - how physically close people are
- Power - shared or focused
- Individualism - collective or individual emphasis
- Competitiveness - highly competitive or not
- Structure - very structured and organized, or loose and very flexible

- Thinking - linear or circular logic, or long-term or short-term goals

VERBAL COMMUNICATION

Communication between cultures is basically the same as within a culture. It is the degree of understanding and the impacts of common misunderstandings that create a greater risk to international projects that are less dramatic with domestic projects. All communication consists of both verbal and nonverbal cues to transmit encoded messages to a receiver who must interpret the message through their own cultural biases to understand that message.

Verbal communication, of course, is a language. Language is the first thing that is often realized as a barrier between cultures. Every culture has its own language even if it is a modification of another language through slang, technical terms, or other adaptations. For example, there are many confusing meanings between Americans and the British over the same words, each using a common language. In some cases, though, there may not be a common language.

In addition, many languages contain multiple forms that can lead to problems if not understood and applied in the proper fashion. Social stature is often measured by the formality and titles used in the very first words spoken or written in a project proposal. Mistakes here can insult the receiver and terminate a project immediately. In some cultures there are words that are used when addressing a man and other words for addressing a woman or a child. Misusing these words can create a range of responses from humor to disgust—all at your expense to your credibility as a project manager.

So the first challenge to the project manager is to decide on a common language to create the project documentation. Ideally the project manager will be able to converse in whatever foreign language is required for better communication. Many nations are much further ahead of the United States when it comes to being multilingual. For example, business managers in Denmark are generally fluent in at least six different languages! As you can imagine, interpreters are becoming more important in the business sector. The translation of many terms and even common phrases must be run through a quality-control process.

NONVERBAL COMMUNICATION

Nonverbal communication takes on an important role in many cultures outside of the American culture. In fact, nonverbal communication is believed to consist of more than 60 percent of any intended message; it is also the most misunderstood part of communication, leading to great project problems. Nonverbal communication is also called metacommunications, paralinguistics, second-order messages, the silent language, and, very appropriately, the hidden dimension of language.

Again, every culture places different emphasis on different things. In the Orient, silence following a presentation, rather than applause, is actually a sign of respect for the ideas and wisdom of the speaker as the audience contemplates the information. Likewise, an American will become impatient with prolonged silence and will attempt to get everyone talking again, which is insulting to Orientals.

Nonverbal communication is the best way to communicate emotions, underscoring key points, and controlling the information presented. It takes many forms, but a few common ones include:

- Facial expressions
- Stature
- Gestures
- Eye contact
- Proximity distance between people and things (for example, the way furniture is arranged in an office ... is it welcoming, or not?)

Many authors have written extensively about how to interpret nonverbal cues. Caution must be taken to read the cues in the context of the culture, remembering that cultures are constantly changing so generalizations may no longer match the author's interpretation.

CULTURAL NOISE IN THE COMMUNICATIONS CHANNEL

MANY PROBLEMS WITHIN THE COMMUNICATION CHANNEL COME FROM

- Ethnocentrism - believing one's culture is superior
- False attributes - inserting your cultural interpretations of situations (especially nonverbal) while in a foreign context.
- Stereotyping
- Decorum - nonverbal behavior, proper time and place for certain subjects, taboo subjects never discussed, and protocol.

OVERCOMING THE BARRIERS REQUIRES ACTION THROUGH

- thorough preparation (studying, anticipation, contingency planning)
- study your feedback (absence is also feedback in itself)
- active listening in multicultural setting
- putting data into environmental and cultural contexts
- remaining polite but not ingratiating
- focusing on building relationships and trust for this and future projects

NEGOTIATION CROSS CULTURES

The key to success in negotiation is through personal relationships and persuasion using common values and goals. When conflict arises, it is important to study the situation and determine the real source of the conflict. Understanding the values of the other culture in order to know better what they are feeling is one of the most important factors in a conflict. Select a location for the meeting and establish acceptable agendas and ground rules in advance.

During negotiations, listen and speak carefully while looking for all the cues. Use everyone on your negotiation team to watch from different angles, miss nothing, and confer frequently during breaks to discuss what is really being transmitted for your choice of action.

NEGOTIATION TECHNIQUES

- Paradigm shift where you consciously flip your way of thinking to look at all angles and possibilities
- Brainstorming options and comparing to come up with an optimal and mutually acceptable solution.
- Fuzzy logic techniques to look into the gray areas to find better solutions and overcome obstacles.

CONFLICT RESOLUTION

- Confrontation = Win / Lose
- Smoothing = Agree to disagree
- Avoiding = Withdraw from conflict
- Bargaining = Splitting the difference or meeting halfway
- Problem solving = Facing issues together for a solution

COMMON NEGOTIATION TACTICS

- Personal attack
- Ultimatums
- Good cop / bad cop
- Walk-out threat
- Piling on = last-minute "add-on items".
- Playing dumb (effort to gain more time)
- Bluff
- Information dump (hide bad news in details)

ETHICS AND LEGALITIES

Ethics are the commonly shared organizational values that define correct behavior and determine to control incorrect behavior. Every culture has its own ethics and every corporation, as its own culture, has its own ethical code. Today, in dealing with a variety of cultural values, laws, and ethical codes the international project has a much more difficult problem determining the right course for project decisions.

Acceptable behavior norms are understood by all in every culture for:

- Self-interest versus organization
- Financial gains
- Efficiency
- Relationships
- Society responsibility
- Morality and belief systems
- Laws

The Project Management Institute has created a professional code of ethics for project management professionals (PMP), and failure to follow this international professional code can lead to dismissal. The key points of the PMP Code are:

- Truthful representations of yourself and your work to PMI and to your customers.
- Reporting any violations witnessed to PMI.
- Maintaining customer confidentiality (unless unlawful) and focusing on customer objectives in work.
- Avoiding conflicts of interest.
- Promoting professional ethics including support to any investigation.

Today, some corporations accept a social responsibility to do the right thing regardless of cost, while others may see a more important obligation to prevent financial losses as for their shareholders' best interests.

A project manager can receive sources of ethical behavior from many directions: her own cultural bias, the foreign culture where the project resides, laws of different countries, the PMI, and her own corporate policies. Is there a way to make international decisions easier?

LEGALITY

The legal systems of different countries vary extensively and this area should not be taken for granted by any project manager. Foreign laws may be much stricter and carry extreme penalties; in other situations, the laws may be without teeth.

The United States realized the problems and created the Foreign Corrupt Practices Act in 1977 to police US companies dealing in unethical practices in foreign countries—primarily in the payment of bribes to foreign officials. The Securities and Exchange Commission (SEC) is responsible for enforcement, and violations carry stiff penalties—$2 million fine to corporation, and each individual faces $200,000 fine and up to five years imprisonment. Still, critics cite that the law leaves a great deal of interpretation as to what constitutes a bribe and what is commonly accepted business practice with foreign governments. It does require standard corporate accounting practices, reports submitted to the SEC, and audits for all assets in a foreign country to identify irregularities in assets that may be transferred as bribes.

GLOBAL PROJECT MANAGER COMPETENCY

There are several forces that drive organizations to develop competency for international project management:

- **Markets** - global branding, smarter global customers focusing on better and tailored products
- **Competition** - domestic markets shrinking and international competition easily enter to compete with every company
- **Technology** - improved communications make many international operations possible and more profitable than ever before
- **Cost Savings** - production and presence overseas can provide lower costs to local foreign customers through avoidance of tariffs and reduced unit costs using local supply chains and production facilities
- **Government** - some governments reward local presence that induce corporations to establish partnerships or establish presence in foreign companies
- **Relationship Management** - corporations must establish and encourage positive relationships with customers, suppliers, partners, and operations on a worldwide scale upon entry into the international market place.

Corporations are usually at one stage of international exposure and development

- **Domestic company** - focused on domestic market with strong domestic knowledge, possible export/import involvement, focus on cross-functional teams, and international strategy for market changes is entry or withdraw from foreign markets
- **International (Multinational) Company** - domestic home market and international markets on a parity, moves toward global company to build international customer relationships, focus is upon cross-cultural teams, and international strategy for market changes is reprioritizing resources between foreign operational units
- **Global Company** - focus is on serving one worldwide market, customizing products to fit local cultural norms, and management focusing upon international branding, and international strategy for market changes is a central strategic center supporting nearly autonomous foreign business unit operations through a free-flowing information network.

The future competitive advantage for corporations dealing in international endeavors or working with a foreign partnership focuses squarely on the management skills dealing across multiple cultures by project or program managers. The goal is a professional integrator that can transcend corporate and cultural boundaries to solve problems efficiently, and to keep projects on track. Key skills to develop and emphasize in training are:

- **Communications skills** - including foreign language, cultural interpretations, and nonverbal
- **Personality** - adaptable, analytical, open minded, empathetic
- **Motivation** - corporation must make foreign assignments and training a boost for career
- **Family** - personal support and adaptive to live in foreign assignments when required
- **General skills** - maintaining broad outlooks, juggle contradictions, experience "hands-on" in international teams and assignments, emotionally stable, can implement risk management

SPECIFIC SKILLS FOR INTERNATIONAL PROJECTS:

- Leadership in chaos situations - ability to "think outside the box" and operating in uncertainty
- Ability to adapt "best practices" to fit a cultural situation by understanding the various contexts and completing detailed analysis of the culture
- Understanding of the historical perspectives from all angles that is often a critical basis in decision making in many cultures and can be used to sell new methods if affiliated with a historical link
- Developing subordinates into leaders and sharing power especially to present a diverse leadership perspective to all shareholders
- Focus on performance measurement for success versus relying on traditional management rules or procedures from domestic experience for success

CHAPTER REVIEW

1. During project implementation the client interprets a clause in the contract to mean that he is entitled to a substantial refund for work recently completed. You review the clause and disagree with the client's conclusion. As the project manager which of the following actions should be taken?
   A. Disregard the customer's conclusion and continue to process invoices regardless of interpretations and disputes.
   B. Advise the customer that ambiguous information in contracts is always interpreted in favor of the contractor.
   C. Immediately correct the clause to remove any possible misinterpretation by the customer.
   D. Document the dispute and refer to the provisions of the contract that address.

2. Before reporting a perceived violation of an established rule or policy, the project manager should:
   A. Determine the risks associated with the violation
   B. Ignore the violation until it actually affects the project results
   C. Convene a committee to review the violation and determine the appropriate response
   D. Ensure there is a reasonably clear and factual basis for reporting the violation

3. You are ready to enter a negotiating session with a group that is from Russia. The Russians have been known to be aggressive and assertive people who like to talk much more than they like to listen. To earn your bonus, you must not be at a disadvantage in your negotiations with them. Therefore, you must concentrate on:
   A. Active listening
   B. Earning the trust on the other side of the negotiating table
   C. Seating arrangements in the negotiating room
   D. Setting and following strict time limits at each step of the negotiating process

4. A person's negotiating skills and temperament certainly are influenced by his/her culture. However, other factors, such as education and experience are, also at work and over time, an individual who is living in a culture that is different from his or her own may take on characteristics of the new culture. This person may behave from a new frame of reference. With respect to negotiation, this illustrates the importance of
   A. Always looking at those with whom you are negotiating as members of a particular cultural group
   B. Becoming overly dependent on cultural knowledge as the cornerstone for all negotiations
   C. Recognizing that cultural stereotyping should be used as a starting point for all international negotiations
   D. Moving beyond cultural stereotyping and seeing people as individuals with unique personality traits and experiences

5. You are the project manager and responsible for quality audits. You have been accused of being a fanatic because of your practice of conducting not one, but multiple, quality audits on a project. Which one of the following types of audits is not an example of a quality audit?
   A. Internal
   B. System
   C. Baseline
   D. Scope

6. You are managing the development of a highly controversial project. Today you called a team meeting and explained the project objectives to the team and several members stood up and left citing philosophical objections to the project. You chased them down the hall trying to convince them to work on the project and explained that you would use the best quality management plan available for this work. One of the team members stopped abruptly and demanded to know what the purpose of such a plan would be. You explained that the objective of any quality management plan is to
   A. Create some regulations to govern the project
   B. Ensure that process adjustments are made in a timely fashion
   C. Improve quality in every aspect of project performance
   D. Ensure that the scope management plan is followed

7. As a project manager, you know that the most important activity to ensure stakeholder satisfaction is
   A. Documenting the requirements
   B. Communication reports
   C. Maintaining a proper work breakdown structure
   D. Ensuring the staff is happy

8. As a project manager you are responsible for maintaining and ensuring integrity for all of the following except?
   A. Personal integrity
   B. Project integrity
   C. Product integrity
   D. Integrity of others

ANSWERS

1. D - PMI PMP Code of Professional Conduct.
2. D - PMI PMP Code of Professional Conduct.
3. A - PMI PMP Code of Professional Conduct.
4. D - PMI PMP Code of Professional Conduct.
5. D - PMI PMP Code of Professional Conduct.
6. C - PMI PMP Code of Professional Conduct.
7. A - PMI PMP Code of Professional Conduct.
8. D - PMI PMP Code of Professional Conduct.